THE
TENDER MERCIES
of
THE LORD

COMFORT IN OUR LORD'S TENDER CARE

❦

FOR THE GLORY OF THE LORD
Pastor Scott Markle

Shepherding the Flock Ministries
7971 Washington St. ❖ Melvin, MI 48454
(810) 378-5323
www.shepherdingtheflock.com

The Tender Mercies of the Lord:
Comfort in Our Lord's Tender Care
by Pastor Scott Markle

Printed in the United States of America

ISBN 9780615954424

Shepherding the Flock Ministries
7971 Washington St.
Melvin, MI 48454
(810) 378-5323
www.shepherdingtheflock.com

DEDICATION

First and foremost,
To the Lord my God,
Whose compassions never have
And never will fail me,
Whose gentle grace is all-sufficient for me,
And whose tender mercies ever surround me.
"Great is Thy faithfulness."

Furthermore,
To the members of Melvin Baptist Church,
Who are ever in and upon my heart,
For whom my heart is ever burdened
That our Lord God of all grace and mercy might
Establish you, strengthen you, and settle you,
Until Christ be perfectly formed in you.

TABLE OF CONTENTS

PREFACE

Casting all your care upon him;
for he careth for you.

1 Peter 5:7

Oh, brethren, what an amazing truth! The Lord our God and heavenly Father, the eternal, almighty God of heaven and earth, truly cares for us who are His own dear children. Indeed, He cares for us with the gentleness of tender love and with the multitude of tender mercies. As sinners before Him, we are not worthy of such tender love and of such tender mercies. Rather, as sinners we are worthy only to receive the outpouring of His fierce and fiery wrath against us. Yet out of the overflowing abundance of His goodness and grace, the Lord our God and heavenly Father pours out the multitude of His tender love, mercies, compassions, and care upon us.

Certainly, the Lord our God and heavenly Father does rebuke and chasten us who are His children when we walk in sinful disobedience and stubborn rebellion against Him. (Hebrews 12:7) Yet He always does this in the tenderness of His love and mercy. Thus in Proverbs 3:11-12 the instruction and assurance is given, "*My son, despise not the chastening of the LORD; neither be weary of his correction: for whom the LORD loveth he correcteth; even as a father the son in whom he delighteth.*" Yes, as many as He loves with fatherly love, He rebukes and chastens through tender love; and this He does "*for our profit, that we might be partakers of his holiness.*" (Hebrews 12:10)

Certainly also, the Lord our God and heavenly Father does prove and try the character of our faith through fiery trials of affliction. "*For thou, O God, hast proved us: thou hast tried us, as silver is tried.*" (Psalm 66:10) Yet throughout the midst of these trials, He is ever with us in tender love and mercy to strengthen us, help us, and uphold us. (Isaiah 41:10) Always it is His loving, tender desire, not that these trials of affliction should overcome us and destroy us, but that they should purify us from spiritual dross and develop us unto spiritual maturity.

Always it is our Lord's loving, tender desire that the trying of our faith should produce the spiritual characteristic of enduring patience within our hearts. (James 1:2) Furthermore, it is our Lord's loving, tender desire that this characteristic of enduring patience should have its perfect work in our lives, in order that we might grow unto spiritual maturity and Christ-likeness. (James 1:3) Finally, it is our Lord's loving, tender desire that the trying of our faith, *"being much more precious than of gold that perisheth, though it be tried with fire, might be found unto praise and honour and glory at the appearing of Jesus Christ."* (1 Peter 1:7)

Oh, how this truth concerning the tender mercies of our Lord ought to fill our hearts with spiritual confidence, courage, and comfort. Herein we may find the spiritual confidence to set our whole-hearted trust and hope upon our loving, tender Lord. Herein we may find the spiritual courage to continue without fainting in the service of our loving, tender Lord. Herein we may find the spiritual comfort to rise up with fullness of joy in the fellowship of our loving, tender Lord.

Who is a God like unto the Lord our God, who delights in showing mercy unto His own? (Micah 7:18) He is our loving Lord. He is *"the Father of mercies, and the God of all comfort."* (2 Corinthians 1:3) He is the good Shepherd of His sheep. In gentleness and tenderness, He leads us in the right way. Even when He must lead us for our spiritual good *"through the valley of the shadow of death,"* He will provide us with the spiritual courage of His loving presence and with the spiritual comfort of His tender mercies. (Psalm 23:4) Surely His goodness and mercy shall follow us all the days of our lives. (Psalm 23:6)

Dear reader, it is my earnest prayer that you may indeed find spiritual confidence, courage, and comfort through the message of this small book. It is my prayer that the Lord may use the message of this book to direct the focus of your heart upon Himself.

For the excellency of the knowledge of Christ Jesus our Lord, Abiding in Christ, and Christ in us, Pastor Scott Markle

Chapter 1

❧

THE NATURE
OF
OUR LORD'S TENDER MERCIES

*The LORD is gracious,
and full of compassion;
slow to anger, and of great mercy.
The LORD is good to all:
and his tender mercies
are over all his works.*

Psalm 145:8-9

O h, brethren, Psalm 145:8-9 presents a wonderful truth for us. The Lord's tender mercies are over all His works. They are poured out with abundance upon all His works. According to Ephesians 2:10, we who have received God's gracious gift of salvation through faith in the Lord Jesus Christ are the very *workmanship* of God our heavenly Father. *"For we are his workmanship, created in Christ Jesus unto good works, which God hath before ordained that we should walk in them."*

In addition, Philippians 1:6 reveals that the Lord our God and heavenly Father, who hath begun His good *work* in us, *"will perform it until the day of Jesus Christ."* At this very time, He is continually working in us *"both to will and to do of his good pleasure."*

15

(Philippians 2:13) At this very time, He is continually working in us *"that which is well pleasing in his sight."* (Hebrews 13:21)

We are the workmanship of the Lord our God, and the Lord our God continues to work in and through us. *"And his tender mercies are over all his works."* Oh, what a blessed, marvelous, wonderful truth this is to us! We ourselves are a part of His works. Even now our Lord is at work in our hearts and lives. Therefore, the tender mercies of the Lord our God are over *us*. Yea, they are poured out with overflowing abundance upon *us*. Oh, how our hearts need a greater understanding of this truth!

A Yearning and Longing of Heart

Yet what are these tender mercies of the Lord that He pours out abundantly upon us? How are they to be understood? The two English words, "tender mercies," are a translation of one Hebrew word. In fact, that Hebrew word is so intensive that it cannot be adequately translated by any one English word. It is a word of intense emotion. It is a word of great tenderness and compassion. It is a word that expresses the warmest care and the deepest concern for another. It is a word that expresses a yearning and longing on behalf of another. It is a word that expresses a yearning and longing from the deepest levels of the heart.

The literal picture behind these words, "tender mercies," has to do with the bowels. In ancient times people represented various emotions by referring to their bowels, or gut area. They did this because many emotions are physically felt in our gut and stomach area. At times we speak the same way to-day. When we are nervous, we speak of butterflies in our stomach. When we are worried over something, we may become sick to our stomach. When we are suddenly frightened, we may speak of that fright as being so powerful that it was like a punch to our stomach.

Even so, when we are yearning and longing over someone, where do we feel it? We feel it in our gut and stomach area. This is the very idea of the phrase "***bowels of mercies***" in Colossians 3:12 and of the phrase "***bowels of compassion***" in 1 John 3:17. This is the very feeling of yearning and longing that is conveyed to us in the phrase, "***The tender mercies of the LORD.***"

The Reality of Divine Emotion

The Lord our God and heavenly Father is not like many earthly fathers, who do not know how to show tenderness and compassion toward their children. The Lord our God is a tender heavenly Father. He is full of compassions toward us. He is sensitive toward us. Just as a loving father tenderly provides compassion and comfort to his children, "***so the LORD pitieth them that fear him.***" (Psalm 103:13)

Brethren, the same kind of feeling, the same kind of yearning and longing that a mother might have toward her injured child – that is the same kind of feeling

17

that the Lord our God feels toward us. The references
to our Lord God's emotions in God's Holy Word are
not simply expressions. They describe the true feelings of our Lord God's heart. He really does feel
these things emotionally. Such emotions are a very
part of His divine nature.

The Lord our God really does feel a yearning and a
longing in heart over the lost that they might be saved.
He really does feel a yearning and a longing in heart
over His backslidden people that they might return unto
Him in repentance. He really does feel a yearning
and a longing in heart over His faithful people that
they might walk in intimate fellowship with Him.
Oh, brethren, our Lord's yearning and longing over
us, our Lord's tender mercies toward us, are true
emotions that move Him to the depth of His heart.

Understanding through Biblical Example

Two Biblical examples of this yearning and longing
in heart may help us to acquire a better sense of these
things. First, when Joseph first saw his beloved brother
Benjamin after Joseph's many years in Egypt, he
yearned over his brother in this way. Genesis 43:30
reads, "***And Joseph made haste; for his bowels did
yearn upon his brother: and he sought where to weep;
and he entered into his chamber, and wept there.***"

The yearning of Joseph's bowels (or, as we might
say today – the yearning of Joseph's heart) moved
him to weep over his brother. Even so, the yearning

of our Lord's heart moves Him to *weep* over us. True, the Lord our God does not have physical eyes like a man with which to weep physical tears. Yet, just as we might weep in our spirit and heart without shedding physical tears, even so the Lord our God really does weep in His spirit and in His heart over us.

In a second Biblical example, we see the yearning of a mother over her infant son at a threat to his life. This is seen in a dispute between two harlots that King Solomon, in his great wisdom, was required to judge.

1 Kings 3:16-27 reads, "***Then came there two women, that were harlots, unto the king, and stood before him. And the one woman said, O my lord, I and this woman dwell in one house; and I was delivered of a child with her in the house. And it came to pass the third day after that I was delivered, that this woman was delivered also: and we were together; there was no stranger with us in the house, save we two in the house.***"

"***And this woman's child died in the night; because she overlaid it*** [that is – rolled over it]***. And she arose at midnight, and took my son from beside me, while thine handmaid slept, and laid it in her bosom, and laid her dead child in my bosom. And when I rose in the morning to give my child suck, behold, it was dead: but when I had considered it in the morning, behold, it was not my son, which I did bear.***"

"And the other woman said, Nay; but the living is my son, and the dead is thy son. And this said, No; but the dead is thy son, and the living is my son. Thus they spake before the king. Then said the king, The one saith, This is my son that liveth, and thy son is the dead: and the other saith, Nay; but thy son is the dead, and my son is the living. And the king said, Bring me a sword. And they brought a sword before the king. And the king said, Divide the living child in two, and give half to the one, and half to the other."

"Then spake the woman whose the living child was unto the king, for her bowels yearned upon her son, and she said, O my lord, give her the living child, and in no wise slay it. But the other said, Let it be neither mine nor thine, but divide it. Then the king answered and said, Give her the living child, and in no wise slay it: she is the mother thereof."

Oh, the yearning of a mother for her child! So much was the yearning of this mother for her child that she was willing to give him up to another in order to keep him alive. This is the kind of yearning that the Lord our God has toward us. No, our Lord most certainly will not give us up to the devil. Yet He does yearn over us so much that He will do all that is according to His nature in order to give us life, yea even to give us life more abundantly. Thus He proclaimed in Isaiah 49:15, *"Can a woman forget her sucking child, that she should not have compassion on the son of her womb? Yea, they may forget, yet will I not forget thee."*

20

Brethren, the yearning of Joseph upon his brother and the yearning of this mother upon her baby boy give us an apt illustration of our Lord God's yearning and longing, of His tender mercies, upon us. We are His chosen generation, whom He has called "***out of darkness into his marvelous light.***" (1 Peter 2:9) We are His peculiar people, His special treasure, His dear children.

He has engraved us who are His own upon the very palms of His hands. (Isaiah 49:16) Therein He carries us close to His bosom in tender love and mercy. Therein He keeps us so that no individual and no force is able to pluck us out of His hand. (John 10:28-29) We truly are dear to His heart. We truly are the apple of His eye. (Psalm 17:8)

Chapter 2

❧

THE FULLNESS
OF
OUR LORD'S TENDER MERCIES

*It is of the LORD'S mercies
that we are not consumed,
because his compassions fail not.
They are new every morning:
great is thy faithfulness.*

Lamentations 3:22-23

We have learned already from Psalm 145:9 that our Lord's tender mercies "*are over all his works.*" Now, from other passages of God's Holy Word, we shall see the fullness of that truth.

Ever from Eternity Past

From Psalm 25:6 we learn that our Lord's tender mercies "*have been ever of old.*" In that verse the man of God David cried unto the Lord, "*Remember, O LORD, thy tender mercies and thy lovingkindnesses; for they have been ever of old.*" As far back as we might look in history, even unto the very creation of the heaven and the earth, we will find the tender mercies of the Lord our God. Yea, even before time began in the creation, even unto the far reaches of eternity past, the tender mercies of the Lord our God are there.

25

This is true because the Lord our God is full of mercy by His very nature. In Exodus 34:6 He revealed Himself unto Moses on Mount Sinai. Thus we read, "*And the LORD passed by before him, and proclaimed, The LORD, The LORD God, merciful and gracious, longsuffering, and abundant in goodness and truth.*" Even so, Psalm 116:5 declares, "*Gracious is the LORD, and righteous; yea, our God is merciful.*" In like manner, Psalm 103:8 declares, "*The LORD is merciful and gracious, slow to anger, and plenteous in mercy.*" So then, just as He Himself is from eternity past in His eternal existence, even so His tender mercies are "*ever of old*" as an integral part of His eternal nature.

Never Failing into Eternity Future

Yet it is not necessary that we look only into the past to find the tender mercies of the Lord our God. We may also expect His tender mercies now, and ever also into the future. In Lamentations 3:22-23 the prophet Jeremiah declared, "*It is of the LORD'S mercies that we are not consumed, because his compassions fail not. They are new every morning: great is thy faithfulness.*"

In this passage the word "compassions" translates the same Hebrew word as the phrase "tender mercies" in the Psalms. Herein we have the same intensive, emotional, tender, compassionate, warm, deep yearning of the Lord our God toward us. Herein we are told that the compassions (the tender mercies) of the

Lord our God are *unfailing*. Not only have our Lord's tender mercies and compassions been ever of old in eternity past, but they also never fail into eternity future.

It is also important for us to notice that these ideas are Biblically expressed in the plural. They are the tender mercie**s** (plural) and the compassion**s** (plural) of the Lord our God. Herein we are not looking in particular upon the merciful nature of the Lord our God. Rather, we are here looking upon the river of tender mercie**s** (plural) and compassion**s** (plural) that flow unto us who are His dear children, one after the other, out of our Lord God's merciful nature.

The Lord our God is full of mercy by nature. Flowing out of the heart of His nature are His tender mercies and compassions, one after another, after another, after another. This river of our Lord's tender mercies and compassions is ever flowing with abundance. It never ceases. It never has ceased to flow, and it never shall cease to flow. In fact, forty-one times throughout God's Holy Word we hear the proclamation that our Lord's mercy "***endureth for ever.***" The river of our Lord's tender mercies and compassions will never dry up.

The tender mercies and compassions of the Lord our God will never run out. There will always be enough. There will always be enough for each and every one of us. There will always be enough for all of our needs, for all of our circumstances, and for all of our troubles.

There will always be enough for each and every one of us, for all of these things, for all time. The tender mercies and compassions of the Lord our God "*fail not.*"

Ever Flowing as a Fresh River

Furthermore, the river of our Lord's tender mercies and compassions is always flowing as a *fresh* river. "*It is of the LORD'S mercies that we are not consumed, because his compassions fail not. They are new every morning: great is thy faithfulness.*" The tender mercies and compassions of the Lord our God are *renewed* unto us *every* morning. There is not one new morning in which our Lord's tender mercies and compassions are not flowing toward us in a fresh manner.

There is not one morning that we can awake and say, "Ah, the river of the Lord's tender mercies and compassions has ceased." Indeed, there is not one morning that we can awake and say, "Ah, the river has ceased to be refreshed and is now growing stagnant." Not only does the river of our Lord's tender mercies and compassions never dry up, it also never stagnates. It is ever a refreshed river. It is never a stagnant swamp. It is always refreshed with fresh compassions and tender mercies.

Certainly we could live on yesterday's tender mercies and compassions from the Lord our God, for they are that great. Yet our merciful Lord God does not require this of us. In order to demonstrate His great love and kindness toward us, our Lord personally renews the river of His tender mercies and compassions unto us every new morning. Oh, what a marvelous wonder is the loving kindness of the Lord our God unto us!

Ever Sufficient for All Our Need

Yet the question may arise – Are the ever of old, ever flowing, never failing, ever renewed compassions and tender mercies of the Lord our God adequate for all my need? Are they *all-sufficient* for *me* and for *my* needs? To this question the answer of heaven rings back through the true and holy Word of God by the inspiration of God the Holy Spirit – Yes, the compassions and tender mercies of the Lord are absolutely and abundantly sufficient for you and for all your needs, in any way, in any shape, in any form!

Yes, brethren, our Lord's compassions and tender mercies are adequate and all-sufficient for us. Yea, Psalm 119:156 proclaims, "***Great are thy tender mercies, O LORD: quicken me according to thy judgments.***" Our Lord's tender mercies are indeed great. Yea, they are infinitely great, even as the Lord our God is infinitely great. They not only can meet all our need; they are truly *greater* than all our need.

"***The LORD is merciful and gracious, slow to anger, and <u>plenteous</u> in mercy. He will not always chide: neither will he keep his anger for ever. He hath not dealt with us after our sins; nor rewarded us according to our iniquities. For as the heaven is high above the earth, <u>so great</u> is his mercy toward them that fear him. As far***

29

as the east is from the west, so far hath he removed our transgressions from us. Like as a father pitieth his children, so the LORD pitieth [has tender mercy upon] *them that fear him. For he knoweth our frame; he remembereth that we are dust. As for man, his days are as grass: as a flower of the field, so he flourisheth. For the wind passeth over it, and it is gone; and the place thereof shall know it no more. But the mercy of the LORD is from everlasting to everlasting upon them that fear him, and his righteousness unto children's children.*" (Psalm 103:18-17)

This was the assurance of David, "*the servant of the LORD,*" in Psalm 36:5, "*Thy mercy, O LORD, is in the heavens; and thy faithfulness reacheth unto the clouds.*" Again this was the assurance of David in Psalm 57:10, "*For thy mercy is great unto the heavens, and thy truth unto the clouds.*"

Yet again this was the assurance of David in Psalm 86:13-17, "*For great is thy mercy toward me: and thou hast delivered my soul from the lowest hell. O God, the proud are risen against me, and the assemblies of violent men have sought after my soul; and have not set thee before them. But thou, O Lord, art a God full of compassion, and gracious, longsuffering, and plenteous in mercy and truth. O turn unto me, and have mercy upon me; give thy strength unto thy servant, and save the son of thine handmaid. Shew me a token for good; that they which hate me may see it, and be ashamed: because thou, LORD, hast holpen me, and comforted me.*"

Even so, we also should walk with the assurance that the Lord our God is "***full of compassion***" and "***plenteous in mercy.***" Yea, we should walk with the assurance that our Lord's compassions and tender mercies are indeed great toward us, and that He will abundantly deliver us, strengthen us, help us, and comfort us thereby.

THE TENDER MERCIES OF OUR LORD

Are over All His Works

Are Poured Out unto Us
His Dear Children

Are Ever of Eternity Past

Flow from His Merciful Nature

Fail Not into Eternity Future

Are Ever Flowing as a Fresh River

Are All-Sufficient for All Our Need

Chapter 3

❧

PARTAKING
OF
OUR LORD'S TENDER MERCIES

Let us therefore come boldly
unto the throne of grace,
that we may obtain mercy,
and find grace to help in time of need.

Hebrews 4:16

Brethren, the only reason that we do not enjoy our Lord's tender mercies and do not find them to be more than adequate for all our need is because we are not partaking of them. We live in a spiritually dry and thirsty land. Our lives are spiritually dry and thirsty lives. Our hearts are spiritually dry and thirsty hearts. Every day we are in need of our Lord God's living water.

Thus the Lord our God causes the river of His living water to flow forth from His throne of grace, ever renewed every new day to meet our daily need. Yet if we never dip into the river of our Lord's living water, we shall still be spiritually dry and thirsting. No matter how much of that living water flows by us, if we do not dip into that water and partake of it, we shall never enjoy its refreshment, its help, and its blessing.

Our Great High Priest

So then, how do we partake of this ever flowing, never failing, ever of old, yet every day renewed river of our Lord's tender mercies? The answer is given in Hebrews 4:14-16, wherein we are instructed, "***Seeing then that we have a great high priest, that is passed into the heavens, Jesus the Son of God, let us hold fast our profession. For we have not an high priest which cannot be touched with the feeling of our infirmities; but was in all points tempted like as we are, yet without sin. Let us therefore come boldly unto the throne of grace, that we may obtain mercy, and find grace to help in time of need.***"

God the Son, our Lord and Savior Jesus Christ, is our great High Priest. He is our great High Priest, "***that is passed into the heavens.***" As God the Son, He is the all-sufficient One. Yea, He is all-sufficient to meet all our need. In addition, as our great High Priest, He is even now "***touched with the feeling of our infirmities.***" He is not a High Priest who simply *was* touched (past tense). The first half of Hebrews 4:15 is given in the present tense. Our Lord and Savior Jesus Christ is our great High Priest, who is *presently* touched with the *present* feeling of our *present* infir-mities. This is the truth of our Lord's tender mercies and compassions toward us. He *presently* yearns and longs over us and with us.

Yet how could He be touched with the feeling of our infirmities? How can He understand where we live and what we must suffer? Our Lord and Savior Jesus Christ understands because He lived upon this earth as one of us. No, he did not live as a sinner like us. He never committed sin. He *"was in all points tempted like as we are, yet without sin."* Yet our Lord did live as one of us upon this earth. As John 1:14 declares, He *"was made flesh, and dwelt among us."*

Even so, Hebrews 2:17-18 declares, *"Wherefore in all things it behoved him to be made like unto his brethren, that he might be a merciful and faithful high priest in things pertaining to God, to make reconciliation for the sins of the people. For in that he himself hath suffered being tempted, he is able to succour them that are tempted."* He suffered. He died. He understands.

With all of this context, Hebrews 4:16 reveals how we may dip into the river of our Lord's tender mercies and compassions. It gives the instruction, *"Let us therefore* [because we have such a great High Priest] *come boldly unto the throne of grace, that we may obtain mercy, and find grace to help in time of need."* Even so, Psalm 86:5 proclaims, *"For thou, Lord, art good, and ready to forgive; and plenteous in mercy unto all them that call upon thee."* Yet again Psalm 145:18 proclaims, *"The LORD is nigh unto all them that call upon him, to all that call upon him in truth."*

37

Humble, Dependent Prayer

How do we dip into the tender mercies of the Lord our God? How do we obtain them in order to quench our thirst and meet our need? We do so by calling upon the Lord in humble, dependent prayer. We do so by coming boldly and continually unto our Lord God's throne of grace through prayer, asking Him to pour out His tender mercies upon us and to meet our need thereby.

We do so by bowing before our Lord and calling upon our Lord, saying – "Oh, Lord my God, I live in a dry and thirsty land. I am a dry and thirsty soul. My soul thirsteth for Thee. My flesh longeth for Thee. I know that all other ground is parched, dry, and empty. Oh, Lord, I know that Thou alone art the Source of living water, the only One who can quench my soul's thirsting. Please, Lord, out of the abundance of Thy tender mercies, meet my need."

This was the prayer of David in Psalm 4:1, "*Hear me when I call, O God of my righteousness: thou hast enlarged me when I was in distress; have mercy upon me, and hear my prayer.*" This was the prayer of David in Psalm 6:1-4, "*O LORD, rebuke me not in thine anger, neither chasten me in thy hot displeasure. Have mercy upon me, O LORD; for I am weak: O LORD, heal me; for my bones are vexed. My soul is also sore vexed: but thou, O LORD, how long? Return, O LORD, deliver my soul: oh save me for thy mercies' sake.*"

This also was the prayer of David in Psalm 25:6-7, *"**Remember, O LORD, thy tender mercies and thy lovingkindnesses; for they have been ever of old. Remember not the sins of my youth, nor my transgressions: according to thy mercy remember thou me for thy goodness' sake, O LORD.**"* To this David added in Psalm 25:16-17, *"**Turn thee unto me, and have mercy upon me; for I am desolate and afflicted. The troubles of my heart are enlarged: O bring thou me out of my distresses**."*

Again this was the prayer of David in Psalm 9:13, *"**Have mercy upon me, O LORD; consider my trouble which I suffer of them that hate me, thou that liftest me up from the gates of death**."* This was the prayer of David in Psalm 27:7, *"**Hear, O LORD, when I cry with my voice: have mercy also upon me, and answer me**."* This was the prayer of David in Psalm 30:10, *"**Hear, O LORD, and have mercy upon me: LORD, be thou my helper**."* This was the prayer of David in Psalm 31:9, *"**Have mercy upon me, O LORD, for I am in trouble: mine eye is consumed with grief, yea, my soul and my belly**."*

Yet again this was the prayer of David in Psalm 56:1-3, *"**Be merciful unto me, O God: for man would swallow me up; he fighting daily oppresseth me. Mine enemies would daily swallow me up: for they be many that fight against me, O thou most High. What time I am afraid, I will trust in thee**."* This was the prayer of David in Psalm 57:1, *"**Be merciful unto me, O God, be merciful unto me: for my soul trusteth in thee: yea,*** *in the shadow of thy wings will I make my refuge, until these calamities be overpast.*" Finally, this was the prayer of David in Psalm 86:3, "*Be merciful unto me, O Lord: for I cry unto thee daily.*"

The Fear of the Lord

However, there is a prerequisite for our prayers to be effective. In Psalm 103:11 the truth is revealed, "*For as the heaven is high above the earth, so great is his mercy toward them that fear him.*" The great abundance of our Lord's tender mercies is poured out upon "*them that fear him.*" In order for our prayers to be effective, we must walk in the fear of the Lord. Our character and our conduct must be governed by the fear of the Lord.

Yet what does it mean to walk in the fear of the Lord and to be governed by the fear of the Lord? First, it means to be gripped deeply in heart with reverential awe toward the Lord. Even so, Psalm 33:8 declares, "*Let all the earth fear the LORD: let all the inhabitants of the world stand in awe of him.*" In like manner, Psalm 89:7 declares, "*God is greatly to be feared in the assembly of the saints, and to be had in reverence of all them that are about him.*"

Second, to walk in the fear of the Lord means to walk daily in faithful obedience unto the commandments of our Lord. Even so, Psalm 103:17-18 declares, "*But the mercy of the LORD is from everlasting to everlasting upon them that fear him, and his righteousness unto*

***children's children; to such as keep his covenant,
and to those that remember his commandments to
do them.***" Again Psalm 112:1 declares, "***Praise ye the
LORD. Blessed is the man that feareth the LORD,
that delighteth greatly in his commandments.***" Yet
again Psalm 128:1 declares, "***Blessed is every one
that feareth the LORD; that walketh in his ways.***"

Third, to walk in the fear of the Lord means to cleave
whole-heartedly with the commitment of loving service
unto the Lord. Even so, in Deuteronomy 10:12 Moses
proclaimed, "***And now, Israel, what doth the LORD thy
God require of thee, but to fear the LORD thy God,
to walk in all his ways, and to love him, and to serve
the LORD thy God with all thy heart and with all
thy soul.***" To this he added in verse 20, "***Thou shalt
fear the LORD thy God; him shalt thou serve, and to
him shalt thou cleave, and swear by his name.***" In
like manner, in 1 Samuel 12:24 Samuel proclaimed,
"***Only fear the LORD, and serve him in truth with
all your heart: for consider how great things he
hath done for you.***"

Fourth, to walk in the fear of the Lord means to come
humbly unto repentant confession of our sins against
the Lord. Even so, Psalm 28:13-14 declares, "***He that
covereth his sins shall not prosper: but whoso confesseth and forsaketh them shall have mercy. Happy
is the man that feareth alway: but he that hardeneth
his heart shall fall into mischief.***" Again Proverbs
16:6 declares, "***By mercy and truth iniquity is purged:
and by the fear of the LORD men depart from evil.***"

Fifth, to walk in the fear of the Lord means to wait patiently with trusting hope in the mercifulness of our Lord. Even so, Psalm 33:18-22 declares, "***Behold, the eye of the LORD is upon them that fear him, upon them that hope in his mercy; to deliver their soul from death, and to keep them alive in famine. Our soul waiteth for the LORD: he is our help and our shield. For our heart shall rejoice in him, because we have trusted in his holy name. Let thy mercy, O LORD, be upon us, according as we hope in thee.***"

The Assurance of Outpoured Mercy

So then, if we will walk in the fear of the Lord, we may have full assurance of faith that our Lord will pour out the abundance of His compassions and tender mercies upon us. Then we may claim the assurance of Psalm 147:11, "***The LORD taketh pleasure in them that fear him, in those that hope in his mercy.***"

Then we may claim the assurance of Psalm 31:19-20, "***Oh how great is thy goodness, which thou hast laid up for them that fear thee; which thou hast wrought for them that trust in thee before the sons of men! Thou shalt hide them in the secret of thy presence from the pride of man: thou shalt keep them secretly in a pavilion from the strife of tongues.***"

Then we may claim the assurance of Psalm 34:7-10, "***The angel of the LORD encampeth round about them that fear him, and delivereth them. O taste and see that the LORD is good: blessed is the man that***

trusteth in him. O fear the LORD, ye his saints: for there is no want [no lack] **to them that fear him. The young lions do lack, and suffer hunger: but they that seek the LORD shall not want any good thing.**"

Then we may claim the assurance of Psalm 145:18-20, "**The LORD is nigh unto all them that call upon him, to all that call upon him in truth. He will fulfil the desire of them that fear him: he also will hear their cry, and will save them. The LORD preserveth all them that love him: but all the wicked will he destroy.**"

43

Chapter 4

❧

BUILDING OUR ASSURANCE
ON
OUR LORD'S TENDER MERCIES
(PART 1)

Have mercy upon me, O God,
according to thy lovingkindness;
according unto the multitude
of thy tender mercies
blot out my transgressions

Psalm 51:1

S o then, in what specific areas may we build our assurance upon the tender mercies of the Lord our God? Already we have learned that our Lord's tender mercies are more than sufficient to meet all of our need. Yet does the Lord our God in His Holy Word give us any specific examples in this matter? Certainly He has given us examples. Indeed, He has recorded in His true and holy Word the real life cases and real life prayers of men of God of old. Just as these men of God of old founded their assurance for answered prayer upon the tender mercies of the Lord, even so may we.

The Word of God is filled with the real life cases of real life people who went through real life needs and real life problems, and who found the Lord to be a real life God to meet their real life needs. Even so, James

5:10-11 declares, "***Take, my brethren, the prophets, who have spoken in the name of the Lord, for an example of suffering affliction, and of patience. Behold, we count them happy which endure. Ye have heard of the patience of Job, and have seen the end of the Lord; that the Lord is very pitiful, and of tender mercy.***"

"The tender mercies of the Lord our God" is not just a nice phrase that we use in order to make ourselves feel good. God forbid! Rather, the tender mercies of the Lord our God are real to life. They are real life mercies to help us in our real life needs. Even so, in 1 Corinthians 1:3-4 the blessing is pronounced and the assurance is provided, "***Blessed be God, even the Father of our Lord Jesus Christ, the Father of mercies, and the God of all comfort; who comforteth us in all our tribulation, that we may be able to comfort them which are in any trouble, by the comfort wherewith we ourselves are comforted of God.***"

By nature the Lord our God is "***the Father of mercies, and the God of all comfort.***" By nature He pours forth His merciful compassions and gracious comforts unto us in all our cases of tribulation. Thus we ourselves *can* find our Lord's tender mercies real to meet our real needs, even as men of God of old found them real to meet their real needs. For what then did these men of God of old pray, and for what then may we also pray, according to the tender mercies of the Lord our God?

48

We may pray with assurance
according to our Lord's tender mercies –
That He will bring eternal salvation to lost souls.

❧

When John the Baptist was a newborn infant, Zacharias his father prophesied before the Lord. In Luke 1:76 Zacharias looked upon his son John and said, "***And thou, child, shalt be called the prophet of the Highest: for thou shalt go before the face of the Lord to prepare his ways***." John the Baptist was born as the forerunner of the Lord Jesus Christ, to preach repentance and to prepare the way before the Lord.

Yet why did God the Father send a forerunner before the face of His Son, the Lord Jesus Christ, to prepare the way of His earthly ministry among the nation of Israel? Luke 1:77 reveals the reason, saying, "***To give knowledge of salvation unto his people by the remission of their sins***." Through what then was this knowledge of salvation and this remission of sins given? The opening portion of verse 78 gives answer, saying, "***Through the tender mercy of our God***."

Yet this passage reveals even more that was provided "***through the tender mercy of our God***." Luke 1:78-79 continues, saying, "**W***hereby the dayspring from on high* [that is – the Lord Jesus Christ our Savior] *hath visited us, to give light to them that sit in darkness and in the shadow of death, to guide our feet into the way of peace***."

49

It is "***through the tender mercy of our God***" that He brought forth the knowledge of eternal salvation and the eternal remission of sins unto us spiritually lost sinners. It is "***through the tender mercy of our God***" that He sent "***the dayspring from on high***," God the Son, the Lord Jesus Christ, to be our eternal Savior. Indeed, the fact that any lost soul may be eternally saved from his or her sins is all through the tender mercies of the Lord our God.

If you yourself have been drawn to the place wherein you received the Lord Jesus Christ through faith as your personal and eternal Savior from sin, then you were drawn to that place through the tender mercies of the Lord our God. The eternal redemption, eternal salvation, eternal regeneration, and eternal justification of your eternal soul is all through the Lord's tender mercies.

Even so, Titus 3:3-7 declares, "***For we ourselves also were sometimes foolish, disobedient, deceived, serving divers lusts and pleasures, living in malice and envy, hateful, and hating one another. But after that the kindness and love of God our Saviour toward man appeared, not by works of righteousness which we have done, but according to his mercy he saved us, by the washing of regeneration, and renewing of the Holy Ghost; which he shed on us abundantly through Jesus Christ our Saviour; that being justified by his grace, we should be made heirs according to the hope of eternal life***."

Again Ephesians 2:1-7 declares, "***And you hath he quickened, who were dead in trespasses and sins; wherein in time past ye walked according to the course of this world, according to the prince of the power of the air, the spirit that now worketh in the children of disobedience: among whom also we all had our conversation in times past in the lusts of our flesh, fulfilling the desires of the flesh and of the mind; and were by nature the children of wrath, even as others. But God, who is rich in mercy, for his great love wherewith he loved us, even when we were dead in sins, hath quickened us together with Christ, (by grace ye are saved;) and hath raised us up together, and made us sit together in heavenly places in Christ Jesus: that in the ages to come he might shew the exceeding riches of his grace in his kindness toward us through Christ Jesus.***"

Yet again 1 Peter 1:3-5 declares, "***Blessed be the God and Father of our Lord Jesus Christ, which according to his abundant mercy hath begotten us again unto a lively hope by the resurrection of Jesus Christ from the dead, to an inheritance incorruptible, and undefiled, and that fadeth not away, reserved in heaven for you, who are kept by the power of God through faith unto salvation ready to be revealed in the last time.***"

On the other hand, if you have not yet come to that place of faith in the Lord Jesus Christ as your personal Savior, then right now the Lord God Himself is drawing you and calling you in His tender mercy. In

His tender mercy, He is calling at this very moment for you to repent of your sinfulness before Him and to receive the Lord Jesus Christ as your personal and eternal Savior from sin.

Oh, how I beseech you – Heed the call of God's tender mercy! Come through faith unto the Lord Jesus Christ for eternal salvation from your sin! Call upon Him in faith to be your Savior! Indeed, "***the same Lord over all is rich*** [in mercy and grace] ***unto all that call upon Him. For whosoever shall call upon the name of the Lord shall be saved***." (Romans 10:12-13)

Furthermore, brethren, if you are burdened for a lost soul, and if you are longing and praying for his or her salvation, there is a great assurance available to you. In His tender mercies toward that same lost soul, the Lord our God and Savior is yearning over him or her even more than you are. Indeed, the Lord our God and Savior has a far greater burden for any and every lost soul than we may ever have.

In the multitude of His tender mercies, the Lord our God and Savior is earnestly longing to give unto every lost soul the knowledge of their salvation and the remission of their sins. According to 1 Timothy 2:4, the Lord our God and Savior desires for "***all men to be saved, and to come unto the knowledge of the truth***." Even now, at this very moment, the Lord our God and Savior, through His tender mercy, is drawing upon their hearts and is calling them unto faith in His Son for salvation.

52

**We may pray with assurance
according to our Lord's tender mercies –
That He will forgive and cleanse our sins,
and will restore us unto His fellowship.**

Brethren, at the very moment of our faith in the Lord Jesus Christ as our eternal Savior, we were eternally saved and made a part of God's family. Yet, although we are even now the children of God, we still sin against the Lord our God and heavenly Father. Yes, we are the very children of God. Yet we are often disobedient children.

We know this to be true, but what shall we do about it? The truth of God's Holy Word teaches that we must confess our sins unto the Lord and forsake them through His power. Proverbs 28:13 states, "*He that covereth his sins shall not prosper: but whoso confesseth and forsaketh them shall have mercy.*" We must repent of our sins with a broken and contrite heart, earnestly and humbly seeking our Lord's forgiveness and cleansing.

Ah, but now arises the question – Will the Lord our God and heavenly Father forgive us of our sinfulness and cleans us of our unrighteousness? Will He restore us unto a place of fellowship with Him? Will He give unto us the power for victory over our sins? Oh yes, brethren, according to the multitude of His tender mercies He *will*!

If we come unto the Lord our God with a broken and contrite heart over our sin, He will neither despise us nor turn us aside. Even so, Psalm 51:17 declares, "***The sacrifices of God are a broken spirit: a broken and a contrite heart, O God, thou wilt not despise.***" If we confess our sins with a heart of humble repentance and ask for forgiveness and cleansing, the Lord our God will be faithful and just to grant our request. Even so, 1 John 1:9 declares, "***If we confess our sins, he is faithful and just to forgive us our sins, and to cleanse us from all unrighteousness.***"

If we will repent of our sinful thoughts and our sinful ways, our merciful Lord *will* have abundant mercy upon us. If we will return unto Him with a broken heart of repentance, our merciful Lord *will* abundantly pardon us. Even so, in Isaiah 55:6-7 the promise is given, "***Seek ye the LORD while he may be found, call ye upon him while he is near: let the wicked forsake his way, and the unrighteous man his thoughts: and let him return unto the LORD, and he will have mercy upon him; and to our God, for he will abundantly pardon.***"

If we come unto our Lord with a broken, contrite, and humble spirit of repentance, praying – "Oh, Lord, please forgive me and cleanse me of my sinfulness. Please restore me unto Thy fellowship. Please change and transform the character of my heart. Please create in me a clean heart and renew in me a right spirit." – According to the multitude of His tender mercies, He *will* do it.

In Psalm 51:1 David prayed unto the Lord, saying, *"Have mercy upon me, O God, according to thy lovingkindness; according unto the multitude of thy tender mercies blot out my transgressions."* Herein David prayed for the forgiveness of his sins. Yet upon what foundational assurance did he lift up this prayer for forgiveness? He prayed with assurance according to the multitude of the Lord's tender mercies. In fact, the entire rest of this psalm flows out of this verse.

Every request that David made throughout this psalm, he founded upon the multitude of the Lord's tender mercies. This was his foundational assurance when he prayed for cleansing from sin in verse 2, saying, *"Wash me throughly from mine iniquity, and cleanse me from my sin."* Again this was his foundational assurance when he prayed for transformation of heart in verse 10, saying, *"Create in me a clean heart, O God; and renew a right spirit within me."* Yet again this was his foundational assurance when he prayed for restoration to fellowship in verses 11-12, saying, *"Cast me not away from thy presence; and take not thy holy spirit from me. Restore unto me the joy of thy salvation; and uphold me with thy free spirit."*

All of these requests were founded upon the multitude of our Lord's tender mercies. Even so, since the river of our Lord's tender mercies is ever flowing, never ceasing, and every day renewed unto us, we also can found our request for forgiveness, for cleansing, for transformation, and for restoration upon the multitude of our Lord's tender mercies.

Oh, brethren, we sin so often against the Lord our God. Yet *every time* that we come unto Him with a broken and contrite heart, He *will* forgive us of our sins and *will* cleanse us from our unrighteousness. *Every time*, according to the multitude of His tender mercies, He will *immediately* restore us unto the place of perfect fellowship with Him and will *immediately* begin the process of creating in us a clean heart and of renewing in us a right spirit. This is the assurance of the ever flowing, never failing, ever of old, yet every day renewed river of our Lord's tender mercies toward us.

"The LORD is merciful and gracious, slow to anger, and plenteous in mercy. He will not always chide: neither will he keep his anger for ever. He hath not dealt with us after our sins; nor rewarded us according to our iniquities. For as the heaven is high above the earth, so great is his mercy toward them that fear him. As far as the east is from the west, so far hath he removed our transgressions from us. Like as a father pitieth his children, so the LORD pitieth them that fear him." (Psalm 103:8-13)

"To the Lord our God belong mercies and forgivenesses, though we have rebelled against him." (Daniel 9:9) Indeed, the Lord our God is gracious and merciful, and will not turn His face from us, if we return unto Him with a broken and contrite heart of repentance. (2 Chronicles 30:9) Thus with full assurance of faith, we may join in the prayer of David from Psalm 25:11, saying, *"For thy name's sake, O LORD, pardon mine iniquity; for it is great."*

He *will* abundantly pardon our iniquity, "*because he delighteth in mercy.*" (Micah 7:18) "*He will turn again, he will have compassion upon us; he will subdue our iniquities; and thou wilt cast all their sins into the depths of the sea.*" (Micah 7:19). There *is* forgiveness with our Lord. Therefore, let us hope in Him, "*for with the LORD there is mercy, and with him is plenteous redemption.*" (Psalm 130:7)

Chapter 5

BUILDING OUR ASSURANCE
ON
OUR LORD'S TENDER MERCIES
(PART 2)

Return, O LORD, deliver my soul: oh save me for thy mercies' sake.

Psalm 6:4

Yes, the Lord our God is "*the Father of mercies, and the God of all comfort.*" (2 Corinthians 1:3) There is no one like unto the Lord our God, "*that pardoneth iniquity, and passeth by the transgression*" of His people. (Micah 7:18) There is no one like unto the Lord our God, who keeps covenant and mercy with His servants that walk before Him with all their heart. (1 Kings 8:23) There is no one like unto our Lord God, who is good, "*ready to pardon, gracious and merciful, slow to anger, and of great kindness,*" and plenteous in mercy unto all that call upon him. (Nehemiah 9:17; Psalm 86:5)

Thus we *can* find our Lord's tender mercies real to meet our real needs. Even so, we have learned in the previous chapter that we may pray with assurance according to our Lord's tender mercies – that He will bring eternal salvation to lost souls and that He will forgive and cleanse our sins, and will restore us unto His fellowship. Yet there is more.

61

**We may pray with assurance
according to our Lord's tender mercies –
That He will relieve us
from the corruption of our own sins.**

Brethren, as we have previously noted, we do often sin against the Lord our God and heavenly Father. Because of this, we must reckon with our Lord God's principle of sowing and reaping. Concerning this principle Galatians 6:7-8 proclaims, "***Be not deceived; God is not mocked: for whatsoever a man soweth, that shall he also reap. For he that soweth to his flesh shall of the flesh reap corruption; but he that soweth to the Spirit shall of the Spirit reap life everlasting.***"

As we walk in sin, we are sowing to our sinful flesh. In Galatians 6:7-8 the Lord our God reveals His universal principle for this life. As we sow to our sinful flesh, we shall reap spiritual corruption in this life. We cannot avoid this principle of God. It does indeed apply to us who are the children of God. In fact, Galatians 6:7-8 was written, not to the lost, but to the saved. The corruptive consequences of our sowing to our sinful flesh will surely find us out and take hold upon us.

Oh, what a dreary principle this is to us. When we honestly consider how much we have sown to our sinful flesh, this principle begins to weigh heavily upon our hearts. Oh, how very much corruption we must be required to reap – because of how very much sowing to our sinful flesh we have done. Yet there is a place where we may find *relief* from the corruptive consequences of our own sinful ways. There is a place of hope for us sinners.

That place of relief and hope is the fruitful ground and ever flowing river of our Lord's tender mercies. According to the multitude of His tender mercies, our Lord will even relieve us and preserve us from the corruptions of our own sin and carnality. In the midst of our carnal and corrupt sowing, our merciful Lord will sow the abundance of His mercy and grace.

If we have sown unto our sinful flesh, and yet have come unto the Lord our God with a broken and con- trite heart over that sinful sowing, He will sow His abundant grace in that very same field. Then over time our Lord's abundant grace will grow up over the corruptive consequences of our sin. We will still face these corruptive consequences, but our Lord's abun- dant grace will grow up over them and will bring forth gracious blessing out of negative consequence.

This was the very focus of David's prayer in Psalm 40:11-12. *"**Withhold not thou thy tender mercies from me, O LORD: let thy lovingkindness and thy truth continually preserve me. For innumerable evils have compassed me about:** [Why?] **mine iniquities have taken hold upon me, so that I am not able to look up; they are more than the hairs of mine head:***

therefore my heart faileth me." David had sown unto his sinful flesh, and he was now reaping the corruption.

Yet He he continued his prayer in verses 13-17, saying, "*Be pleased, O LORD, to deliver me: O LORD, make haste to help me. Let them be ashamed and confounded together that seek after my soul to destroy it; let them be driven backward and put to shame that wish me evil. Let them be desolate for a reward of their shame that say unto me, Aha, aha. Let all those that seek thee rejoice and be glad in thee: let such as love thy salvation say continually, The LORD be magnified. But I am poor and needy; yet the Lord thinketh upon me: thou art my help and my deliverer; make no tarrying, O my God*."

As David recognized in verse 12, his iniquities had taken hold upon him. He was bound by the chords and chains of his own sins. He was in bondage to his own sins. He was surrounded and overwhelmed by the corruptive consequences of his own sins. These corruptive consequences were more than he could number. As he focused his attention upon them, his heart fainted within him. As he focused his attention upon these innumerable corruptive consequences of his own sins, he could not look up with hope.

Yet he prayed for the Lord to preserve him. Yet he prayed for the Lord to deliver him. Yet he prayed for the Lord to help him. Yet he prayed for the Lord to relieve him from these corruptive consequences. So then, upon what foundational assurance did David

pray for these things? The answer is revealed in Psalm
40:11. David prayed upon the foundational assurance
of the multitude of the Lord's tender mercies.   When
he focused his attention upon the corruptive consequences of his sins, he could not look up with hope.
Yet when he looked up unto his merciful Lord through
prayer, he was filled with hope.

In like manner, the man of God Asaph prayed concerning the whole of God's people Israel. In Psalm
79:1-4 he cried unto God, "***O God, the heathen are
come into thine inheritance; thy holy temple have
they defiled; they have laid Jerusalem on heaps. The
dead bodies of thy servants have they given to be
meat unto the fowls of the heaven, the flesh of thy
saints unto the beasts of the earth. Their blood have
they shed like water round about Jerusalem; and
there was none to bury them. We are become a reproach to our neighbours, a scorn and derision to
them that are round about us***."

Yet why was this so? Why were God's own people
in such a wretched state? It was because the Lord's
anger had been kindled against them. They had
willfully sinned against Him and had rebelliously continued to walk therein. Therefore, they were reaping
the corruption that they had sown unto themselves by
their own sinful iniquity.

Yet Asaph continued his prayer in verses 5-9, saying,
"***How long, LORD? Wilt thou be angry for ever?
Shall thy jealousy burn like fire? Pour out thy wrath***

***upon the heathen that have not known thee, and upon
the kingdoms that have not called upon thy name.
For they have devoured Jacob, and laid waste his
dwelling place. O remember not against us former
iniquities: let thy tender mercies speedily prevent us:
for we are brought very low. Help us, O God of our
salvation, for the glory of thy name: and deliver us,
and purge away our sins, for thy name's sake.***"

God's people were in a terrible condition. They were
in great trouble. The heathen were destroying God's
people and were defiling His holy land and His holy
temple. The reason was that God's own people had
greatly sinned against Him and had greatly provoked
Him unto righteous anger thereby. This the man of
God Asaph acknowledged.

Yet Asaph asked if the Lord would continue to be
angry forever. Then in answer to his own question,
he expressed the assurance that the Lord his God would
not continue to be angry forever. Thus he prayed that
the Lord would relieve His people from the corruptive consequences of their own sins. The man of God
prayed that the Lord would not continue to remember
their former iniquities. Yea, he prayed that the Lord
would speedily pour out His tender mercies upon His
own people, in order to help them, deliver them, and
relieve them.

Now, it is especially noteworthy that the man of God
Asaph presented his request all for the Lord's name's
sake. He presented his request all for the glory of the

Lord's name. If we are to be relieved from the corruptive consequences of our own sins, our help and hope must be wholly founded upon the tender mercies of the Lord our God. Therefore, when our Lord brings that help and that relief to us, He should get all of the glory. His name alone should be exalted.

Even so, in Psalm 79:10-13 Asaph concluded his prayer, saying, "***Wherefore should the heathen say, Where is their God? Let him be known among the heathen in our sight by the revenging of the blood of thy servants which is shed. Let the sighing of the prisoner come before thee; according to the greatness of thy power preserve thou those that are appointed to die; and render unto our neighbours sevenfold into their bosom their reproach, wherewith they have reproached thee, O Lord. So we thy people and sheep of thy pasture will give thee thanks for ever: we will shew forth thy praise to all generations***."

Yea, we will give Thee thanks, O Lord, and show forth Thy praise because Thou hast relieved us from the corruptive consequences of our own sins; and this Thou hast done according to the multitude of Thy tender mercies. Even so, in Psalm 31:7-8 the man of God David lifted up his thanks and praise unto the Lord, saying, "***I will be glad and rejoice in thy mercy: for thou hast considered my trouble; thou hast known my soul in adversities; and hast not shut me up into the hand of the enemy: thou hast set my feet in a large room***."

Yet why was David in such trouble and adversity at that time? The answer is revealed as David prayed in Psalm 31:9-10, saying, "*Have mercy upon me, O LORD, for I am in trouble: mine eye is consumed with grief, yea, my soul and my belly. For my life is spent with grief, and my years with sighing: my strength faileth because of mine iniquity, and my bones are consumed.*" David's trouble, adversity, and grief at that time were the corruptive consequences of his own iniquity.

Yet upon the foundational assurance of the Lord's tender mercies, David prayed for deliverance from these corruptive consequences. Yea, according to the multitude of the Lord's tender mercies, David knew that the Lord had heard his prayer. He knew that the Lord had considered his trouble. He knew that the Lord would mercifully and graciously deliver him from these corruptive consequences.

In like manner, David prayed with assurance in Psalm 6:1-4, saying, "*O LORD, rebuke me not in thine anger, neither chasten me in thy hot displeasure. Have mercy upon me, O LORD; for I am weak: O LORD, heal me; for my bones are vexed. My soul is also sore vexed: but thou, O LORD, how long? Return, O LORD, deliver my soul: oh save me for thy mercies' sake.*" Furthermore, in Psalm 41:4 David prayed with assurance, saying, "*I said, LORD, be merciful unto me: heal my soul; for I have sinned against thee.*"

In both of these cases, David's soul was weak and sore vexed because of the Lord's rebuke and chastening against his sins. He had committed sin against the Lord. The Lord's righteous anger and hot displeasure was kindled against him. He was reaping the corruptive consequences that he had sown by his sins. Yet upon the foundational assurance of the Lord's tender mercies, David prayed for the Lord to return unto him in fellowship and to deliver him from these corruptive consequences.

Even so, let us pray with assurance according to the multitude of our Lord's tender mercies. Let us pray with assurance that our Lord will cause His anger toward us to cease. (Psalm 85:4) Let us pray with assurance that He will revive us again spiritually that we may rejoice in Him. (Psalm 85:6) Let us pray with assurance that He will show us His mercy and thereby grant us His deliverance. (Psalm 85:7) Let us pray with assurance that our Lord will satisfy us early with His mercy. (Psalm 90:14) Let us pray with assurance that He will make us glad according to the days wherein He had previously afflicted us with corruptive consequences under His chastening hand. (Psalm 90:15)

Chapter 6

❧

BUILDING OUR ASSURANCE
ON
OUR LORD'S TENDER MERCIES
(PART 3)

Hear me, O LORD;
for thy lovingkindness is good:
turn unto me according to the multitude
of thy tender mercies.

Psalm 69:16

Yes, the Lord our God is "*full of compassion, and gracious, longsuffering, and plenteous in mercy and truth*." (Psalm 86:15) "*For the Lord will not cast off for ever: but though he cause grief, yet will he have compassion according to the multitude of his mercies*." (Lamentations 3:31-32) If we return unto Him, He will mercifully turn away the fierceness of His anger from falling upon us, and will heal all our backslidings. (Jeremiah 3:12, 22)

Thus we certainly *can* find our Lord's tender mercies real to meet our real needs. Even so, we have learned in the previous two chapters that we may pray with assurance according to our Lord's tender mercies – that He will bring eternal salvation to lost souls, that He will forgive and cleanse our sins, and will restore us unto His fellowship, and that He will relieve us from the corruption of our own sins. Yet there is still more.

**We may pray with assurance
according to our Lord's tender mercies –
That He will deliver us
through our troubles and tribulations.**

In Psalm 69 David prayed while in a time of great affliction. Indeed, his tribulations and troubles were overwhelming him and drowning him. In Psalm 69:1-2 he described his situation through prayer, saying, "*Save me, O God; for the waters are come in unto my soul. I sink in deep mire, where there is no standing: I am come into deep waters, where the floods overflow me.*"

Oh, brethren, have you ever been in such tribulation that you were overwhelmed in your soul? Have you ever cried so much in the midst of your troubles that your throat hurt and your eyes had no more tears? This was the case for David. In verse 3 he said, "*I am weary of my crying: my throat is dried: mine eyes fail while I wait for my God.*"

Oh, brethren, have you ever been wrongfully accused and wrongfully hated by others? This also was David's case. Again in verse 4 he declared, "*They that hate me without a cause are more than the hairs of mine head: they that would destroy me, being mine enemies wrongfully, are mighty: then I restored that which I took not away.*" David did not have just one enemy that hated him without a cause. He had many such enemies, even more than the hairs of his head.

Oh, brethren, have you ever been hurt and forsaken even by your own family? Consider again David's case from verse 8 – "***I am become a stranger unto my brethren, and an alien*** [a foreigner] ***unto my mother's children***." Oh, brethren, have you ever been so far down that even the "down and outers" see themselves as better off than you are? Consider yet again David's case from verse 12 – "***They that sit in the gate*** [the beggars] ***speak against me; and I was the song of the drunkards***."

Oh, brethren, have you ever suffered reproach for the sake of the Lord's name, for the sake of the Lord's Word, and for the sake of the Lord's ministry? Such was David's case; for he cried unto the Lord in verse 7, saying, "***Because for thy sake I have borne reproach; shame hath covered my face***." Again in verse 9 he cried unto the Lord, saying, "***For the zeal of thine house hath eaten me up; and the reproaches of them that reproached thee are fallen upon me***."

Oh, brethren, have you ever been in such tribulation that your very heart broke with the heaviness? Have you ever been so alone in your troubles that you could find no human friends or comforters? Such also was David's case; for he cried forth in verse 20, "***Reproach hath broken my heart; and I am full of heaviness: and I looked for some to take pity, but there was none; and for comforters, but I found none***."

Brethren, this was David's real life case and real life situation. So then, what did he do? How did he bear up under this great affliction in his life? In verses 13-18 we find the answer. There David proclaimed, "*But as for me, my prayer is unto thee, O LORD, in an acceptable time: O God, in the multitude of thy mercy hear me, in the truth of thy salvation. Deliver me out of the mire, and let me not sink: let me be delivered from them that hate me, and out of the deep waters. Let not the waterflood overflow me, neither let the deep swallow me up, and let not the pit shut her mouth upon me.*"

"*Hear me, O LORD; for thy lovingkindness is good: turn unto me according to the multitude of thy tender mercies. And hide not thy face from thy servant; for I am in trouble: hear me speedily. Draw nigh unto my soul, and redeem it: deliver me because of mine enemies.*"

David was able to bear up under this great affliction by turning and looking unto the Lord his God. In the midst of such great troubles and tribulations, David prayed unto the Lord for deliverance. So then, upon what assurance did David found his prayer? All of his prayer for deliverance from all of his troubles – from his enemies, from the mire, from the overflowing floodwaters, from the tears, and from the pain – the man of God David founded all of his prayer upon the multitude of the Lord's tender mercies.

In verse 16 he prayed, "***Hear me, O LORD; for thy lovingkindness is good: turn unto me according to the multitude of thy tender mercies.***" What brought assurance unto David's heart in his time of great trouble and affliction? What brought assurance unto David's heart that the Lord would hear his prayer, would answer with favor, and would deliver him? That which brought assurance unto David's heart was the great and glorious truth that the Lord his God was a good God, and that the Lord's lovingkindness was good. Yea, that which brought assurance unto David's heart was the great and glorious truth that the Lord has a multitude of tender mercies that are ever flowing unto His people.

Even so, let us also pray with assurance according to the multitude of our Lord's tender mercies. Let us pray with assurance that our Lord will deliver us out of the mire of all our afflictions. Let us pray with assurance that He will preserve us from the deep floodwaters of tribulation. Let us pray with assurance that He will hear us speedily and help us in all our trouble. Let us pray with assurance that He will draw nigh unto our soul and deliver it in the multitude of His tender mercies.

Let us pray with assurance that our Lord will take us up even when everyone else might forsake us. (Psalm 27:10) Let us pray with assurance that He will be our helper so as to turn our mourning into dancing and so as to gird us with joy and gladness. (Psalm 30:10) Let us pray with assurance that He will protect us from the daily oppression of our enemies. (Psalm 56:1-2) Let us pray with assurance that He will deliver our feet from falling. (Psalm 56:13) Let us pray with joyful assurance that our Lord will be our defense and our refuge in the day of trouble. (Psalm 59:16)

Let us pray with the same full assurance with which David prayed in Psalm 86:1-7, saying, "***Bow down thine ear, O LORD, hear me: for I am poor and needy. Preserve my soul; for I am holy: O thou my God, save thy servant that trusteth in thee. Be merciful unto me, O Lord: for I cry unto thee daily. Rejoice the soul of thy servant: for unto thee, O Lord, do I lift up my soul. For thou, Lord, art good, and ready to forgive; and plenteous in mercy unto all them that call upon thee. Give ear, O LORD, unto my prayer; and attend to the voice of my supplications. In the day of my trouble I will call upon thee: for thou wilt answer me***."

Let us pray with the same faith in our merciful Lord with which David prayed in Psalm 109:21-27, saying, "***But do thou for me, O GOD the Lord, for thy name's sake: because thy mercy is good, deliver thou me. For I am poor and needy, and my heart is wounded within me. I am gone like the shadow when it declineth: I am tossed up and down as the locust. My knees are weak through fasting; and my flesh faileth of fatness. I became also a reproach unto them: when they looked upon me they shaked their heads. Help me, O LORD my God: O save me according to thy mercy: that they may know that this is thy hand; that thou, LORD, hast done it***."

Let us pray with the same loving commitment with which the psalmist prayed in Psalm 116:1-8, saying, "*I love the LORD, because he hath heard my voice and my supplications. Because he hath inclined his ear unto me, therefore will I call upon him as long as I live. The sorrows of death compassed me, and the pains of hell gat hold upon me: I found trouble and sorrow. Then called I upon the name of the LORD; O LORD, I beseech thee, deliver my soul.*"

"*Gracious is the LORD, and righteous; yea, our God is merciful. The LORD preserveth the simple: I was brought low, and he helped me. Return unto thy rest, O my soul; for the LORD hath dealt bountifully with thee. For thou hast delivered my soul from death, mine eyes from tears, and my feet from falling.*"

Oh, brethren, no matter what our need may be, no matter how great our need may be, we may pray with full assurance according to the multitude of our Lord's tender mercies. He will help us. The multitude of our Lord's tender mercies was the foundational assurance upon which David prayed for the Lord's help in his time of need. The multitude of our Lord's tender mercies should also be the foundational assurance upon which we pray for help in our time of need.

Chapter 7

BUILDING OUR ASSURANCE
ON
OUR LORD'S TENDER MERCIES
(PART 4)

*Let, I pray thee,
thy merciful kindness be for my comfort,
according to thy word unto thy servant.*

Psalm 119:76

Yes, the Lord our God is the Father of compassionate mercies and the God of all gracious comfort. Yea, in the multitude of His mercies toward us, He forgives all our iniquities, heals all our backslidings, redeems our life from destruction, crowns us with lovingkindness and tender mercies, and satisfies our mouth with good things. (Psalm 103:3-5)

Thus we most certainly *can* find our Lord's tender mercies real to meet our real needs. Even so, we have learned in the previous three chapters that we may pray with assurance according to our Lord's tender mercies – that He will bring eternal salvation to lost souls, that He will forgive and cleanse our sins, and will restore us unto His fellowship, that He will relieve us from the corruption of our own sins, and that He will deliver us through our troubles and tribulations. Yet there is still more.

**We may pray with assurance
according to our Lord's tender mercies –
That He will pour out
the blessings of His goodness upon us.**

In Psalm 25:4-7 David prayed, "*Shew me thy ways, O LORD; teach me thy paths. Lead me in thy truth, and teach me: for thou art the God of my salvation; on thee do I wait all the day. Remember, O LORD, thy tender mercies and thy lovingkindnesses; for they have been ever of old. Remember not the sins of my youth, nor my transgressions: according to thy mercy remember thou me for thy goodness' sake, O LORD.*"

In the final request of verse 7, David asked that the Lord might pour out the blessings of His goodness upon him. Yea, David asked that the Lord might so pour out the blessings of His goodness, that the Lord's goodness might be glorified in the eyes of all around.

Herein David did not pray for some small, private blessings of the Lord's goodness. Rather, he prayed for such amounts of the blessings of the Lord's goodness that all around might see them and might glorify the Lord. In essence, David prayed for an outpouring of the blessings of the Lord's goodness upon him in great, overflowing abundance. How many of us would also desire such an outpouring of the blessings of our Lord's goodness to be upon us?

So then, upon what foundational assurance did David make this request? In verse 6 David revealed the answer, saying, "***Remember, O LORD, thy tender mercies and thy lovingkindnesses; for they have been ever of old.***" To this he added in the closing portion of verse 7, "***According to thy mercy remember thou me for thy goodness' sake, O LORD.***" David prayed for a great and abundant outpouring of the blessings of the Lord's goodness in accord with the multitude of the Lord's tender mercies. David knew that the Lord's mercies were ever flowing from His merciful heart in tenderness and compassion, renewed every morning. Upon that foundational assurance, David made his request.

Even so, we also may make this same request with assurance according to the tender mercies of the Lord our God. We also can pray with full assurance of faith that the Lord might pour out the blessings of His goodness upon us. However, we can only pray this with full assurance if, in fact, the Lord and His goodness will be glorified. If our Lord will not get the glory, then He will not give the blessing.

Therefore, when we pray for the Lord to bless us, we must truly pray from our hearts *for his goodness' sake*. We must truly pray from our hearts that our Lord's goodness will be exalted and honored. Yea, we must have such a heart that when our Lord does bless us, we will be quick to praise Him and His goodness with our lips, and to honor Him and His goodness with our lives. Yes, we can pray with full assurance of faith; but we can only pray with full assurance of faith if we are motivated with a spiritually right heart attitude.

One of the greatest blessings of our Lord's goodness unto us is that of direction and guidance from our Lord's hand. Even so, in Psalm 25:4-5 David prayed, saying, "*Shew me thy ways, O LORD; teach me thy paths. Lead me in thy truth, and teach me: for thou art the God of my salvation; on thee do I wait all the day.*" David desired that the Lord might show him and teach him the way of righteousness. He desired that the Lord might teach him and lead him in and through His truth. This was David's prayer for the blessing of guidance.

So then, upon what foundational assurance did David make this request for the Lord's guidance? As we have already noted, David revealed the answer in verse 6, saying, "*Remember, O LORD, thy tender mercies and lovingkindnesses; for they have been ever of old.*" Even so, we also may pray with full assurance of faith according to the tender mercies of the Lord our God, that He might show us, teach us, and lead us in His way of righteousness through the truth of His Word.

Yea, in this very psalm we are assured that our Lord will so guide us, if we come to Him with a meek and humble heart. Psalm 25:8-9 proclaims, "*Good and upright is the LORD: therefore* [because He is good, upright, and full of tender mercies] *will he teach sinners in the way. The meek will he guide in judgment: and the meek will he teach his way.*"

Our Lord does not require us to be perfect before He will guide us. Rather, according to the multitude of His tender mercies, He promises to teach **sinners** in His way of righteousness. Yet we must be sinners with a broken and contrite heart. We must be sinners with a meek and humble spirit. We must be sinners who are willing to be led out of our sin and unto His righteousness.

We must be sinners of a meek and humble spirit, willing to obey whatever our Lord commands and willing to follow wherever He leads. Even so, Psalm 25:12-14 proclaim, "***What man is he that feareth the LORD? Him shall he*** [the Lord] ***teach in the way that he*** [the Lord] ***shall choose. His soul shall dwell at ease; and his seed shall inherit the earth. The secret of the LORD is with them that fear him; and he will shew them his covenant.***"

We must walk in the fear of the Lord with a meek and humble spirit before Him. This is His requirement unto us. Then according to the multitude of His tender mercies, our Lord will walk with us in the intimacy of His fellowship. Then according to the multitude of His tender mercies, He will guide us in the way of His will. Then according to the multitude of His tender mercies, He will bless us in the abundance of His goodness. This is our assurance in our merciful Lord.

We may trust in the multitude of His tender mercies with all of our heart; for in His abundant mercy, He will deal bountifully with us. (Psalm 13:5-6) In the multitude of His abundant mercy, He will make us to lie down peacefully as sheep in green pastures, and will lead us beside the still waters. (Psalm 23:2) In the multitude of His abundant mercy, He will restore our soul spiritually, and will lead us "*in the paths of righteousness for his name's sake*." (Psalm 23:3) In the multitude of His abundant mercy, He will prepare a table of abundance before us in the very presence of our enemies. (Psalm 23:5) In the multitude of His abundant mercy, He will anoint our head with the oil of gladness, and will cause our cup to run over with the abundance of His blessing. (Psalm 23:5)

Surely His abundant goodness and His tender mercy shall follow us all the days of our lives. (Psalm 23:6) So then, let us pray with assurance, knowing that our merciful Lord God will "*be merciful unto us, and bless us; and cause his face to shine upon us*." (Psalm 67:1). Let us pray with assurance, knowing that He will hold up our goings in His paths, in order that our footsteps might not slip. (Psalm 17:7) Let us pray with assurance, knowing that He causes us to know the way wherein we ought to walk. (Psalm 143:8)

Yea, let us pray with assurance, knowing that He will lift up the light of His countenance upon us. (Psalm 4:6) Let us pray with assurance, knowing that He will put gladness in our heart, "*more than in the time that their corn and their wine increased*." (Psalm 4:7) Let us pray with assurance, knowing that He will make us to "*dwell in safety*," so that we may both lie down and sleep in peace. (Psalm 4:8)

**We may pray with assurance
according to our Lord's tender mercies –
That He will comfort our weary souls
and give us the abundant life.**

❧

Oh, brethren, are you in need of comfort? Are you in need of courage to continue abounding in the work of the Lord? Let us then consider the psalmist's prayer in Psalm 119:75-76 – "*I know, O LORD, that thy judgments are right, and that thou in faithfulness hast afflicted me. Let, I pray thee, thy merciful kindness be for my comfort, according to thy word unto thy servant.*"

Oh, brethren, do you desire to experience the abundant Christian life? Do you desire to be in the place of spiritual usefulness and fruitfulness and in the place of full joy and peace? Let us then consider as the psalmist continued his prayer unto the Lord in verse 77 – "*Let thy tender mercies come unto me, that I may live: for thy law is my delight.*"

Oh yes, we may pray with full assurance according to our Lord's tender mercies, that He will comfort our weary souls and that He will grant us the abundant Christian life. However, we can only pray this with full assurance if we are delighting in the Word and the Law of the Lord. Notice again how the psalmist prayed in Psalm 119:77, "*Let thy tender mercies come unto me, that I may live: for thy law is my delight.*"

89

The psalmist prayed – *Because* I delight in Thy Holy Word, O Lord, not only to read it, study it, learn it, and meditate in it, but also to obey it and live in it – *Because of this I know*, O Lord, that Thou shalt hear my prayer. *Because* I delight in Thy Law, I pray with full assurance according to the multitude of Thy tender mercies, that Thou wilt comfort my weary soul. *Because of this* I pray with full assurance, that Thou wilt give me the courage, the hope, the help, and the peace of the abundant Christian life that I need to continue growing and going forward for Thee.

So then, let us delight ourselves in the law and the commandments of our Lord. Let us view the Word of our Lord's mouth as better unto us "***than thousands of gold and silver***." (Psalm 119:72) Let us take the truth and teaching of our Lord's Word as our heritage forever. (Psalm 119:111) Let us make them the rejoicing and the songs of our hearts in our pilgrimage upon this earth. (Psalm 119:54, 111) Let us set our hope and trust therein. (Psalm 119:42-43)

Let us receive and believe with meekness of heart the truth and teaching of God's Holy Word. Let us meditate day and night therein, and let us submit our hearts and lives to be governed thereby. Let us continually have respect unto the statutes and standards of our Lord's Word. (Psalm 119:117) Let us esteem all the precepts and principles of His Word "***concerning all things to be right***." (Psalm 119:128) Let us hate every way that is contrary thereto.

Let us keep, obey, and follow our Lord's precepts and principles, statutes and standards, commandments and counsels, wisdom and warnings, instructions and admonitions continually with our whole heart forever and ever. (Psalm 119:44, 69) Let us think upon our ways and turn our feet unto the testimonies of our Lord's Word. (Psalm 119:59) Let us incline our hearts to perform our Lord's statutes and standards always unto the end of our lives. (Psalm 119:112) Let us make haste and delay not to keep and obey our Lord's instruction. (Psalm 119:60) Let us not decline our hearts at any time away from our Lord's Word. (Psalm 119:51, 157)

Then we may pray with full assurance of faith that our Lord might comfort our weary souls. Then we may pray with full assurance of faith that our Lord might grant us the abundant Christian life. Then we may pray with full assurance of faith that our Lord might empower us for spiritual usefulness and fruitfulness. Then we may pray with full assurance of faith that our Lord might fill us with His all-surpassing joy and peace. Then we may pray with full assurance of faith according to the multitude of our Lord's tender mercies.

Chapter 8

❧

PRAISING THE LORD
FOR
HIS TENDER MERCIES

Bless the LORD, O my soul:
and forget not all his benefits.

Psalm 103:2

Brethren, this all we may pray with full assurance of faith according to the tender mercies of our Lord – for the salvation of lost sinners, for the forgiveness and cleansing of our sins, for restoration unto our Lord's fellowship and joy, for relief from the consequences of our sins, for help in our time of trouble, for the blessings of our Lord's goodness, for the guidance of our Lord's hand, for comfort to our weary souls, and for the abundant Christian life.

Knowing that this is Biblically true, "*let us therefore come boldly unto the throne of grace, that we may obtain mercy, and find grace to help in time of need.*" (Hebrews 4:16) Yet let us always pray, according to the multitude of our Lord's tender mercies, for the glory of His name and for the honor of His goodness.

Even so, when our Lord pours out these things upon us according to the multitude of His tender mercies, let us then be quick to give thanks unto Him. Yea, let us His people and the sheep of His pasture give thanks

95

unto Him forever and show forth His praise unto all generations. (Psalm 79:13) Let us give thanks unto Him until the day that we die. In addition, let us be certain to praise and to thank the Lord our God before our children and before our children's children. Let us be quick to show unto the following generations all the multitude and all the benefits of our Lord's tender mercies toward us.

Oh, brethren, let us bless the Lord, even as David did in Psalm 103:1-5. Therein David exclaimed, "***Bless the LORD, O my soul: and all that is within me, bless his holy name. Bless the LORD, O my soul, and forget not all his benefits: who forgiveth all thine iniquities*** [the salvation and forgiveness]***; who healeth all thy diseases*** [the restoration and relief]***; who redeemeth thy life from destruction*** [the help in trouble]***; who crowneth thee with lovingkindness and tender mercies*** [the blessing and guidance]***; who satisfieth thy mouth with good things*** [the comfort and abundant life]***; so that thy youth is renewed like the eagle's***."

Let us who seek after our gracious and merciful Lord rejoice and be glad in Him. Let us who love and trust in the deliverance and goodness of our Lord's tender mercies say continually, "***The LORD be magnified***." (Psalm 40:16) Let us praise the name of the Lord our God with a song and magnify Him with thanksgiving. (Psalm 69:30). Let us abundantly utter the memory of His great goodness toward us, according unto the multitude of His tender mercies. (Psalm 145:7)

Let us praise the Lord our God with our whole heart. (Psalm 9:1) Let us show forth all His praise and all His marvelous works. Let us rejoice in the salvation of His tender mercies. (Psalm 13:5) Let us sing unto the Lord because He hath dealt bountifully with us according to the multitude of His tender mercies (Psalm 13:6). Let us sing praise unto Him, "**and not be silent**." (Psalm 30:12). Let us give thanks unto Him forever. Let us praise Him and sing unto Him among the public around us. (Psalm 57:9)

Let us be glad and rejoice in the multitude of our Lord's tender mercies. (Psalm 31:7-8) Let us be glad and rejoice that in tender mercy He considers us in our trouble. Let us be glad and rejoice that in tender mercy He comes close to our soul in adversity. Let us be glad and rejoice that in tender mercy He delivers us from the hand of the enemy. Let us be glad and rejoice that in tender mercy He sets our feet in a large place of abundant blessing.

Let us bless the great goodness of our Lord's tender mercies, saying, "*Oh how great is thy goodness, which thou hast laid up for them that fear thee; which thou hast wrought for them that trust in thee before the sons of men! Thou shalt hide them in the secret of thy presence from the pride of man: thou shalt keep them secretly in a pavilion from the strife of tongues. Blessed be the LORD: for he hath shewed me his marvellous kindness in a strong city.*" (Psalm 31:19-21)

"Be glad in the LORD, and rejoice, ye righteous: and shout for joy, all ye that are upright in heart." (Psalm 32:11) *"Rejoice in the LORD, O ye righteous: for praise is comely for the upright."* (Psalm 33:1) Let the righteous exclaim, *"How excellent is thy loving-kindness, O God! Therefore the children of men put their trust under the shadow of thy wings."* (Psalm 36:7)

Let us sing of the protective power of our Lord's tender mercies. Let us sing aloud of His mercy in the morning, even as they are renewed unto us every morning. (Psalm 59:16) Let us lift up our voice and proclaim, *"Unto thee, O my strength, will I sing: for God is my defence, and the God of my mercy."* (Psalm 59:17) Let us *"sing of the mercies of the LORD for ever."* (Psalm 89:1) Let us open our mouths and make known His faithfulness to all generations.

Let us *"make a joyful noise unto the LORD."* (Psalm 100:1) Let us *"serve the LORD with gladness."* Let us *"come before his presence with singing."* (Psalm 100:2) Let us *"enter into his gates with thanksgiving, and into his courts with praise."* Let us *"be thankful unto him, and bless his name."* (Psalm 100:4) *"For the LORD is good; his mercy is everlasting; and his truth endureth to all generations."* (Psalm 100:5)

"O give thanks unto the LORD, for he is good: for his mercy endureth for ever." (Psalm 107:1) *"Oh that men would praise the LORD for his goodness, and for his wonderful works to the children of men!*

For he satisfieth the longing soul, and filleth the hungry soul with goodness." (Psalm 107:8-9) "*Oh that men would praise the LORD for his goodness, and for his wonderful works to the children of men! And let them sacrifice the sacrifices of thanksgiving, and declare his works with rejoicing*." (Psalm 107:21-22) "*Oh that men would praise the LORD for his goodness, and for his wonderful works to the children of men! Let them exalt him also in the congregation of the people, and praise him in the assembly of the elders*." (Psalm 107:31-32)

"*O praise the LORD, all ye nations: praise him, all ye people. For his merciful kindness is great toward us: and the truth of the LORD endureth for ever. Praise ye the LORD*." (Psalm 117:1-2)

Chapter 9

❧

MOTIVATED
BY
OUR LORD'S TENDER MERCIES

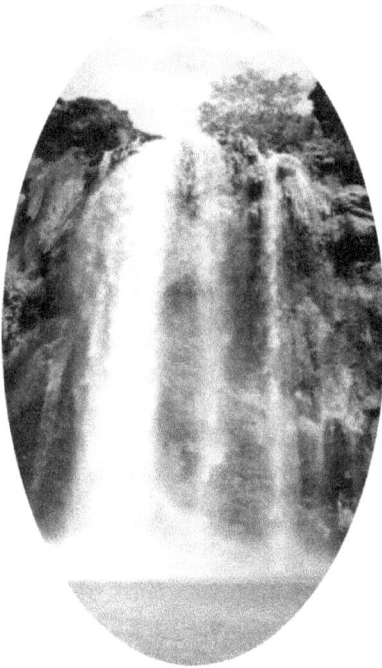

I beseech you therefore, brethren,
by the mercies of God,
that ye present your bodies a living sacrifice,
holy, acceptable unto God,
which is your reasonable service.

Romans 12:1

n Romans 12:1-2 a plea is delivered unto us under the inspiration of God the Holy Spirit – "*I beseech you therefore, brethren, by the mercies of God, that ye present your bodies a living sacrifice, holy, acceptable unto God, which is your reasonable service. And be not conformed to this world: but be ye transformed by the renewing of your mind, that ye may prove what is that good, and acceptable, and perfect, will of God.*"

Herein we are given three instructions. First, we are instructed to present our bodies as a living sacrifice, holy and acceptable unto our Lord. Second, we are instructed not to be conformed unto this present evil world. Third, we are instructed to be transformed into the Lord's image by the renewing of our minds.

Yet all three of these instructions are built upon one foundational motivation. That motivation is presented in the opening phrase of Romans 12:1 – "*I beseech you therefore, brethren, by the mercies of God.*" The foundational motivation for our obedience is the multitude of our Lord's mercies toward us. Brethren, when we truly meditate upon "*the mercies of God,*" then we will be moved and motivated to obedience.

Motivated To Present Ourselves

In the first place, we should be moved and motivated "*by the mercies of God*" to present our bodies as a living sacrifice, holy and acceptable unto the Lord our God. We should be moved and motivated to consecrate and commit ourselves, our whole selves, each and every part of ourselves, unto the Lord our God. Even so, Romans 6:13 proclaims, "*But yield yourselves unto God, as those that are alive from the dead, and your members as instruments of righteousness unto God.*"

Because of the ever flowing, never failing, daily renewed mercies of God, we should be motivated to present ourselves daily as a living sacrifice unto our Lord. In Luke 9:23 our Lord Jesus Christ gave instruction unto His disciples – "*And He said to them all, If any man will come after me, let him deny himself, and take up his cross daily, and follow me.*" Daily our Lord renews His compassions and tender mercies unto us. Therefore, daily we should take up our cross of personal sacrifice unto Him.

Each and every morning of our Christian lives, we should enter the day with this commitment in our hearts and upon our lips – "Dear Lord, because of Thy daily renewed mercies unto me, I deny myself for this day. I present myself as a living sacrifice unto Thee, to live unto Thee, and not unto myself. I will follow Thy will, and none other, for my life today."

Motivated "*by the mercies of God*," we are daily to make a *personal* sacrifice of ourselves unto our Lord. Daily we are to make a personal decision from our own hearts in this matter. Motivated "*by the mercies of God*," we are daily to make a *willing* sacrifice of ourselves unto our Lord. Daily we are to yield ourselves unto the Lord with our own open hands and our own willing heart.

Motivated "*by the mercies of God*," we are daily to make a *complete* sacrifice unto our Lord. We are not simply to present some of our time, some of our wealth, some of our talent, and some of our effort unto the Lord. Rather, we are to yield our whole selves unto our Lord. Daily we are to yield all our thoughts, attitudes, desires, decisions, direction, communication, and conduct unto the Lord our God.

Motivated "*by the mercies of God*," we are daily to make a *living* sacrifice unto our Lord. Daily we are to yield our living unto our Lord, to live day-by-day, moment-by-moment unto Him, and not unto ourselves. Finally, motivated "*by the mercies of God*," we are daily to make a *holy* sacrifice unto our Lord.

105

Daily we are to yield ourselves unto our Lord for the purpose of walking in righteousness and true holiness before Him.

Motivated Not To Be Conformed

In the second place, we should be moved and motivated "*by the mercies of God*" to "*be not conformed to this world.*" Now, the word "conformed" means "to be formed together, to be made into the same form or to be brought into agreement." Thus we are to be moved and motivated not to have the same form as this present evil world or to be in agreement with this present evil world.

"*By the mercies of God,*" we are to be motivated not to think, feel, or behave as this present evil world does. "*By the mercies of God,*" we are to be motivated not to talk or look as this present evil world does. "*By the mercies of God,*" we are to be motivated not to have the same philosophies, priorities, or purposes that this present evil world has. "*By the mercies of God,*" we are to be motivated not to have the same desires, interests, habits, or activities that this present evil world has. "*By the mercies of God,*" we are to be motivated not to make our decisions as this present evil world does.

According to 1 John 2:16 all that is in and of this present evil world involves "*the lust of the flesh, and the lust of the eyes, and the pride of life.*" Thus motivated "*by the mercies of God,*" we are not to be conformed unto such things or to join in fellowship with those who are conformed to such things. Even so, Ephesians 5:11 plainly declares, "*And have no fellowship with the unfruitful works of darkness, but rather reprove them.*"

In like manner, Psalm 1:1 proclaims, "*Blessed is the man that walketh not in the counsel of the ungodly, nor standeth in the way of sinners, nor sitteth in the seat of the scornful.*" Motivated "*by the mercies of God,*" we are not to follow the world's counsels. Motivated "*by the mercies of God,*" we are not to join in fellowship with the world's crowd. Motivated "*by the mercies of God,*" we are not to influence others in the world's conduct.

Motivated To Be Transformed

In the third place, we should be moved and motivated "*by the mercies of God*" to be spiritually transformed by the renewing of our minds. Now, the word "transformed" means "to be formed over, to be distinctly changed in form or character." Thus we are to be moved and motivated to be changed in our spiritual character.

"*By the mercies of God,*" we are to be motivated to be changed from a fleshly character to a spiritual character. "*By the mercies of God,*" we are to be motivated to be changed from an ungodly character to a godly character. "*By the mercies of God,*" we are to be motivated to be changed from an unrighteous character to a righteous character. "*By the mercies of God*," we are to be motivated to be changed from a self-centered character to a God-centered and others-centered character, from a selfish character to a loving character. "*By the mercies of God*," we are to be motivated to be changed from a complaining and critical character to a thankful and kind character.

Motivated "b*y the mercies of God*," we are to be changed from what we are as sinners into the holy and righteous image of our Lord Jesus Christ. Even so, 2 Corinthians 3:18 proclaims, "*But we all, with open face beholding as in a glass the glory of the Lord, are changed into the same image from glory to glory, even as by the Spirit of the Lord*."

Motivated "*by the mercies of God*," we are not simply to be "conformed" to the righteous image of Christ, but to be "transformed" into His image. We are not simply to have a change in outward behavior and to be "conformed" to some outward standard. Rather, motivated "*by the mercies of God*," we are to be changed in the very depths of our hearts and to be "transformed" from the inside to the outside.

Yet how can we thus be "transformed"? Romans 12:2 gives answer, saying, "*But be ye transformed by the renewing of your mind*." Motivated "*by the mercies of God*," we are to have our minds renewed. Motivated "*by the mercies of God*," we are to have our thinking made new. The old carnal thinking of our old sinful flesh will never bring forth a "transformed" life.

Motivated *"by the mercies of God,"* we are to have our minds filled with and governed by the spiritual thinking of God's Holy Spirit and God's holy Word.

If we are to walk like Christ, we must think like Christ. Even so, 1 Corinthians 2:16 reveals to us that *"we have the mind of Christ."* This we have through the indwelling Spirit of God and the engrafted Word of God within us. Yet we must use the mind of Christ that we have been given. Motivated *"by the mercies of God,"* we must allow the Word of Christ to dwell in our hearts richly in all godly wisdom. (Colossians 3:16) Furthermore, motivated *"by the mercies of God,"* we must walk under the holy influence of the indwelling Holy Spirit of God. (Galatians 5:16) Yea, motivated *"by the mercies of God,"* we must be abiding in Christ and allowing Christ to be abiding in us. (John 15:4-5) Then, and only then, shall we be "transformed" into the righteous and holy image of our Lord Jesus Christ.

Chapter 10

❧

WHEN HIS TENDER MERCIES SEEM TO BE CLEAN GONE FOREVER

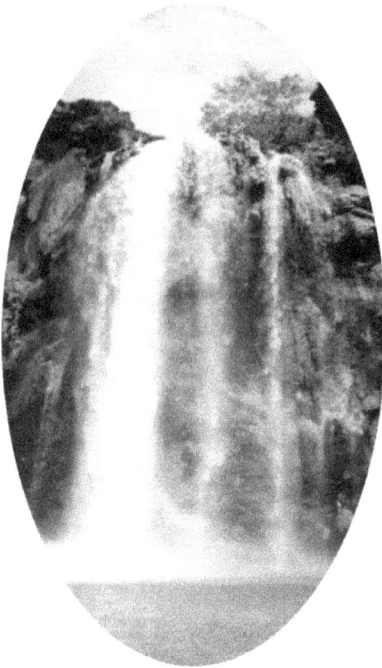

*I had fainted,
unless I had believed to see
the goodness of the LORD
in the land of the living.*

Psalm 27:13

Yet now comes the question, yea even the cry, of some weary and worn soul – What do we do when the tender mercies of the Lord our God seem to have dried up? What do we do when it seems that our Lord has forgotten to be gracious and has shut up His tender mercies from us? What do we do when the dark clouds gather so heavily that we cannot see even a glimpse of a ray of light?

Oh, brethren, what do we do when the storms of life are raging in all of their fury against us? What do we do when we are drowning in the great waves and floodwaters of trouble? What do we do when these waves of trouble mount up to the heavens, and then crash down upon us with all of their weight and power? What do we do when the help and hope of our Lord's tender mercies seem to be clean gone forever? Oh, my beloved brethren, what do we do then?

Oh, brethren, have you ever faced such a time? Might you even now be in such a time? Do you fear that such a time will yet arise for you in the future? I can assure you that others have faced such times before us and have spiritually survived them. Yea, they did more than survive. They passed through these times with spiritual victory.

If they could come through such times with spiritual victory, then so also can we. They did not find the means and the strength to be victorious within themselves. Rather, they found the means and the strength to be victorious in the Lord their God, through the abundant multitude of His tender mercies. So then, we also can find this same means and strength to be victorious through troubled times. The Lord our God has made Himself and His tender mercies available unto us, even as He made Himself and tender mercies available unto them of old.

Furthermore, in His Word the Lord our God has recorded the real life cases of such men of God of old for our learning, for our admonition, for our encouragement, and for our comfort. These men of God of old faced such times of trouble that they literally cried out and said, "Oh, Lord God, where are Thy tender mercies? Are they clean gone forever?" Yet these same men of God of old had victory through these troubled times. In His Word the Lord our God has recorded these real life cases in order that we also might learn from them how to come through such times with spiritual victory.

114

We must cry unto the Lord, remembering His tender mercies of old.

What then do we do in times of raging storm and rising floodwaters? What do we do when our Lord's tender mercies seem to be "***clean gone forever***"? Certainly we must cry unto the Lord in prayer at such times. Such fervent, earnest, heart-felt praying must never be neglected.

Yet we must do more. We must cry unto the Lord our God ***with remembering***. We must cry unto the Lord, remembering what He has done according to the multitude of His tender mercies in past times – yea, in Bible times, and in church history, and in our own church ministry, and in our own family, and in our own past. We must cry unto the Lord ***with remembering***.

In Psalm 77:1-6 the psalmist Asaph declared his case, saying, "*I cried unto God with my voice, even unto God with my voice; and he gave ear unto me. In the day of my trouble I sought the Lord: my sore ran in the night, and ceased not: my soul refused to be comforted. I remembered God, and was troubled: I complained, and my spirit was overwhelmed. Selah. Thou holdest mine eyes waking: I am so troubled that I cannot speak. I have considered the days of old, the years of ancient times. I call to remembrance my song in the night: I commune with mine own heart: and my spirit made diligent search.*"

115

Such was Asaph's real life case. He was in much
trouble from without; and even more so, he was in
much turmoil from within. His soul "*refused to be
comforted.*" His heart was filled with trouble. His
spirit was overwhelmed with turmoil and complaint.
Oh, brethren, consider then as he expressed that turmoil and proclaimed the questions of his own heart
at that time. In Psalm 77:7-9 we hear the psalmist cry
out and ask, "*Will the Lord cast off for ever? And
will He be favourable no more? Is His mercy clean
gone for ever? Doth His promise fail for evermore?
Hath God forgotten to be gracious? Hath He in
anger shut up His tender mercies? Selah.*"

Dear brethren, we are not the only ones who have
come to a place where it appears that the Lord our
God has forgotten us. We are not the only ones who
have come to a place where we feel that our Lord has
forgotten to be gracious, and forgotten to be merciful,
and forgotten to be compassionate, and forgotten to be
tender. Other great men of God of old have come to
this same place, and the Lord our God has recorded
their troubled thoughts and their heart-cries in His
Holy Word. Yea, our Lord has recorded these things
for our learning, that we might relate unto them in our
times of turmoil, and that we might learn the way to
come through the turmoil in spiritual victory.

How then was the man of God Asaph brought through
his turmoil unto victory? As we have already seen,
the psalmist fervently prayed and cried unto the Lord.
Yet he did more than fervently pray and earnestly cry.

He fervently prayed and earnestly cried unto the Lord *with remembering*. In verse 10 the man of God declared, "*And I said, This is my infirmity.*" Asaph recognized that the complaining of his heart was his infirmity. He knew that he ought not to feel the way that he did. He recognized that such thinking was a sinful attitude in the sight of the Lord. Therefore, he humbly acknowledged and confessed his sinful spirit of turmoil and complaining.

Yet how did the man of God Asaph come out of and find spiritual victory over this place of sinful turmoil and complaining? In Psalm 77:10-12 this man of God continued, "*And I said, this is my infirmity: <u>but I will remember</u> the years of the right hand of the most High. <u>I will remember</u> the works of the LORD: <u>surely I will remember</u> thy wonders of old. <u>I will meditate also</u> of all thy works, <u>and talk</u> of thy doings.*"

Even in the midst of his turmoil, this man of God committed himself to remember the wonderful works of the Lord's tender mercies of old. Yea, he committed himself to do more than remember. He committed himself also to meditate upon these wonderful works of the Lord's tender mercies, to think upon them over, and over, and over, and over again. Yea, he committed himself to do even more than remember these wonderful works of the Lord's tender mercies and to meditate upon them. He committed himself even further to gather together with the people of God and to speak among them of the Lord's wonderful and tender mercies.

117

Even so, in Psalm 77:13-14 the man of God Asaph proclaimed, "*Thy way, O God, is in the sanctuary: who is so great a God as our God? Thou art the God that doest wonders: thou hast declared thy strength among the people. Thou hast with thine arm re-deemed thy people, the sons of Jacob and Joseph. Selah*." What then are we to do when the storm is raging around us and the floodwaters are threatening to overcome us? We are to cry unto the Lord our God *with remembering*.

The man of God spoke of remembering the Lord's wondrous works of old. By this he was referring to the Lord's wonderful works of tender mercy. Oh, brethren, when we cry unto the Lord in our times of trouble, let us cry unto Him, *remembering His tender mercies of old*. Rather than worrying over the raging storm and the rising floodwaters of our troubles, let us remember and meditate upon the wonders of our Lord's tender mercies of old. Rather than complaining about *our troubles*, let us talk of all *His wondrous works*.

Let us stop talking ourselves into a state of depression by talking only about our problems. Let us stop talking ourselves into a pit of despair. Let us stop dwelling upon and talking about the turmoil of our hearts. Yes, this turmoil is the true feeling of our hearts. Yet this turmoil of heart is also our infirmity. Let us turn from these feelings of our hearts, and let us look unto the Lord our God. Let us remember His wondrous works of old. Let us meditate upon His

wondrous works of old. Let us talk of all His wondrous works of old. Oh, brethren, let us talk about
the Lord our God, and about His greatness, and about
His goodness, and about His graciousness, and about
His glory.

Furthermore, we must take notice of the one tender
mercy of old that the man of God Asaph mentioned
specifically. It was the redemption that the Lord had
brought unto His people by His almighty arm. In
Psalm 77:15 Asaph proclaimed, ***Thou hast with
thine arm redeemed thy people, the sons of Jacob
and Joseph. Selah***." My friend, have you received
God the Son, the Lord Jesus Christ, through faith as
your personal and eternal Savior from sin and hell?
If you have, then He has wonderfully redeemed you
from your sin with an eternal redemption.

Even so, in the midst of the fiercest storms, let us
ever remember that the Lord our God has eternally
redeemed us according to the multitude of His tender
mercies. In the midst of our darkest hours, let us ever
remember that our Lord and Savior Jesus Christ has
provided eternal redemption for us through His own
precious blood. Let us ever remember the we are
eternally redeemed out of the kingdom of darkness,
out of the bondage of sin, and out of the eternal
judgment of hell. Let us ever remember that we are
eternally redeemed into the kingdom of God's dear
Son as God's own dear children. Oh yes, in times of
raging storms and rising floodwaters, let us fervently
pray and earnestly cry unto the Lord ***with remembering***.

119

We must cry unto the Lord, trusting in His merciful nature

In Isaiah 63:7-14 the prophet Isaiah began by remembering and talking about the Lord's tender mercies of old. Therein he said, "*I will mention the lovingkindnesses of the LORD, and the praises of the LORD, according to all that the LORD hath bestowed on us, and the great goodness toward the house of Israel, which he hath bestowed on them according to his mercies, and according to the multitude of his lovingkindnesses. For he said, Surely they are my people, children that will not lie: so he was their Saviour. In all their affliction he was afflicted, and the angel of his presence saved them: in his love and in his pity he redeemed them; and he bare them, and carried them all the days of old.*"

"*But they rebelled, and vexed his holy Spirit: therefore he was turned to be their enemy, and he fought against them. Then he remembered the days of old, Moses, and his people, saying, Where is he that brought them up out of the sea with the shepherd of his flock? Where is he that put his holy Spirit within him? That led them by the right hand of Moses with his glorious arm, dividing the water before them, to make himself an everlasting name? That led them through the deep, as an horse in the wilderness, that they should not stumble? As a beast goeth down into the valley, the Spirit of the LORD caused him to rest: so didst thou lead thy people, to make thyself a glorious name.*"

Isaiah was remembering the Lord's wonderful works of old. Yet the situation was very different for the prophet Isaiah at that moment. Even so, he voiced the turmoil and the questions of his heart in verse 15, crying out unto the Lord and saying, "***Look down from heaven, and behold from the habitation of thy holiness and of thy glory. Where is thy zeal and thy strength, the sounding of thy bowels and of thy mercies <u>toward me</u>? Are they restrained?***"

Yes, we may remember the Lord's tender mercies of old. Yet what about our case of overwhelming trouble now? Where are the Lord's tender mercies and compassions for us now? Yea, they were in old time; but where are they now? Are they restrained? Have they ceased to flow unto us? At such times of overwhelming trouble, our hearts might cry out unto the Lord as did Isaiah's heart – "Oh, Lord my God, has Thy heart gone cold toward me? Hast Thou rejected me? Hast Thou turned Thy back upon me? Hast Thou cast me aside?"

Yet as the prophet Isaiah asked these questions, he went on to answer them himself; and his answer was to respond with a heart of faith. In Isaiah 63:16 he declared, "***Doubtless*** [without a doubt, with absolute faith and certainty, I know] ***thou art our Father, though Abraham be ignorant of us, and Israel*** [Jacob] ***acknowledge us not: thou, O LORD, art our Father, our Redeemer; thy name is from everlasting***."

Isaiah declared – Oh, Lord my God, I cannot see Thy tender mercies. I cannot see Thy compassions. In the turmoil of my heart, I begin to wonder if they have been restrained. Yet with the answer of faith unto the questioning turmoil of my own heart, I exclaim – **Doubtless**, though everyone else might reject me and forsake me, yea **doubtless**, Thou art my Father. Yea **doubtless**, Thou art my Redeemer. Yea **doubtless**, Thou shalt never, ever forsake me.

Oh, brethren, this is a heart of faith. This is a heart that trusts in the Lord our God. This is a heart that remembers, not only what God has done, **but also who God is**. This is a heart that believes that our Lord is a merciful God by nature, and that He delights in showing mercy. This is a heart that believes that our Lord is still pouring out the abundant multitude of His tender mercies upon His own today. This is a heart that believes the Word and promises of the Lord.

Even so, brethren, we must learn to walk by faith, and not by sight. We must learn to look beyond the raging storm and the rising floodwaters of our lives. We must learn to look, not with the eyes of sight, but with the eyes of faith. Yea, with the eyes of faith, we must learn to look beyond the black clouds that surround us, in order that we might see the glorious light of the Lord our God and Redeemer. We must believe in the Lord our God as heavenly Father, and must whole-heartedly trust in His everlasting love. We must believe in His merciful nature and must trust in His Word of truth and promise unto us.

Even when we cannot see Him or feel Him, we must know the certainty of faith that He is there and that He cares for us. Even though we may have rebelled against Him, and His wrath may be kindled against us, even still we must know with the certainty of faith that He cares for us. Yea, we must know that our heavenly Father chastens us specifically because He loves us and cares for us. *"For whom the Lord loveth he chasteneth, and scourgeth every son whom he receiveth*." (Hebrews 12:6)

Even as the Lord declared unto His backslidden people in Isaiah 54:7-8, the same remains true today. The Lord our God is *"the same yesterday, and to day, and for ever*." (Hebrews 13:8). Therefore, our Lord declares unto His people for all time in Isaiah 54:7-8, *"For a small moment have I forsaken thee; but with great mercies will I gather thee. In a little wrath I hid my face from thee for a moment; but with everlasting kindness will I have mercy upon thee, saith the LORD thy Redeemer*."

Therefore, let us join with the commitment and prayer of the psalmist from Psalm 123:1-3, saying, *"Unto thee lift I up mine eyes, O thou that dwellest in the heavens. Behold, as the eyes of servants look unto the hand of their masters, and as the eyes of a maiden unto the hand of her mistress; so our eyes wait upon the LORD our God, until that he have mercy upon us. Have mercy upon us, O LORD, have mercy upon us: for we are exceedingly filled with contempt*."

Let us join with the prayer, commitment, and assurance of David from Psalm 57:1-3, saying, "*Be merciful unto me, O God, be merciful unto me: for my soul trusteth in thee: yea, in the shadow of thy wings will I make my refuge, until these calamities be overpast. I will cry unto God most high; unto God that performeth all things for me. He shall send from heaven, and save me from the reproach of him that would swallow me up. Selah. God shall send forth his mercy and his truth.*"

Let us join with the commitment of David from Psalm 56:3-4, saying, "*What time I am afraid, I will trust in thee. In God I will praise his word, in God I have put my trust; I will not fear what flesh can do unto me.*" Again let us join with the commitment of David from Psalm 27:1, saying, "*The LORD is my light and my salvation; whom shall I fear? The LORD is the strength of my life; of whom shall I be afraid?*"

Yet again let us join with the assurance of David from Psalm 27:5, saying, "*For in the time of trouble he shall hide me in his pavilion: in the secret of his tabernacle shall he hide me; he shall set me up upon a rock.*" Finally, let us join with the assurance of David from Psalm 27:13-14, saying, "*I had fainted, unless I had believed to see the goodness of the LORD in the land of the living. Wait on the LORD: be of good courage, and he shall strengthen thine heart: wait, I say, on the LORD.*"

Oh, brethren, let us then learn to remember the Lord our God and to meditate upon Him. Let us learn to set our trust and hope in Him, no matter how the storms of life may rage and the floodwaters may rise. Let us believe in the Lord our God and Savior with hope, even when our situation and case appears to leave no room for hope. Let us not be weak in faith. Let us not consider the storm and the darkness around us. Let us not stagger at the truth and the promise of God through unbelief.

Oh, brethren, let us be strong in faith, giving glory to God, and being fully persuaded in our hearts, that what our Lord God has promised us, He is fully willing and able also to perform. Let us remember the multitude of His tender mercies, and let us trust in His merciful heart.

All the way my Savior leads me -
What have I to ask beside?
Can I doubt His tender mercy,
Who thru life has been my Guide?
Heavenly peace, divinest comfort,
Here by faith in Him to dwell!
For I know, what-e'er befall me,
Jesus doeth all things well.

All the way my Savior leads me -
Cheers each winding path I tread,
Gives me grace for every trial,
Feeds me with the living bread.
Thou my weary steps may falter
And my soul athirst may be,
Gushing from the Rock before me,
Lo! A spring of joy I see.

Fanny J. Crosby (1820-1915)

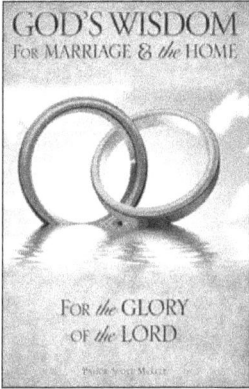

The GOD'S OWN WORD Booklet Series

The "God's Own Word" booklet series is intended to reveal only God's own Word on a particular matter. Each booklet provides a compilation of Biblical passages on a particular subject and categorizes those passages under a set of headings related to that subject. In addition, portions of each passage are highlighted in bold italics in order to point out the parts of the passage that are the most relevant to the subject. In this manner, the reader is instructed *by God's own Word*. I pray that these booklets may spiritually edify, exhort, and encourage your heart.

GOD'S OWN WORD
To Those Who Are Mistreated

Chapter Contents
(63 pages)

Do Good to Those Who Mistreat You
Love Your Enemies
Maintain a Tender Heart and
a Forgiving Spirit
Rejoice When You Suffer
for Christ's Sake
Wait with Patience upon the Lord's
Deliverance
Trust the Lord to Repay Those Who
Mistreat You

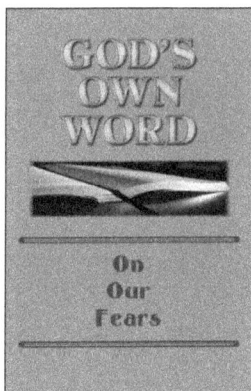

www.ingramcontent.com/pod-product-compliance
Lightning Source LLC
Chambersburg PA
CBHW031321040426
42443CB00005B/177